ROME
THE GREATEST EMPIRE

An illustrated history of power and politics: leadership, war,
conquest, government and the foundation of the modern world

NIGEL RODGERS
Consultant: Dr Hazel Dodge FSA

southwater

For my father

This edition is published by Southwater
Southwater is an imprint of Anness Publishing Ltd
Hermes House, 88–89 Blackfriars Road, London SE1 8HA
tel. 020 7401 2077; fax 020 7633 9499
www.southwaterbooks.com; info@anness.com
© Anness Publishing Ltd 2005

UK agent: The Manning Partnership Ltd, 6 The Old Dairy,
Melcombe Road, Bath BA2 3LR; tel. 01225 478444
fax 01225 478440; sales@manning-partnership.co.uk

UK distributor: Grantham Book Services Ltd
Isaac Newton Way, Alma Park Industrial Estate,
Grantham, Lincs NG31 9SD; tel. 01476 541080
fax 01476 541061; orders@gbs.tbs-ltd.co.uk

North American agent/distributor: National Book
Network, 4501 Forbes Boulevard, Suite 200, Lanham,
MD 20706; tel. 301 459 3366; fax 301 429 5746
www.nbnbooks.com

Australian agent/distributor: Pan Macmillan Australia,
Level 18, St Martins Tower, 31 Market St, Sydney,
NSW 2000; tel. 1300 135 113; fax 1300 135 103
customer.service@macmillan.com.au

New Zealand agent/distributor: David Bateman Ltd
30 Tarndale Grove, Off Bush Road, Albany, Auckland
tel. (09) 415 7664; fax (09) 415 8892

A CIP catalogue record for this book is available
from the British Library.

Publisher: Joanna Lorenz
Editorial Director: Helen Sudell
Editor: Joy Wotton
Designer: Nigel Partridge
Jacket Designer: Steers McGillian Ltd
Illustrator: Peter Bull Art Studio
Production Controller: Darren Price

Previously published as part of a larger volume,
The Rise and Fall of Ancient Rome

1 3 5 7 9 10 8 6 4 2

PICTURE ACKNOWLEDGEMENTS

Ancient Art and Architecture Collection: 36, 97t, 103. **The Art Archive**: 12c, 14l, 14r, 33b, 44t, 45, 49t, 51b, 52t, 55, 58-59, 66t, 70t, 72b, 73t, 75b, 76t, 78, 79, 82, 85, 87b, /Dagli Orti 18t, 20t, 30b, 41b, 42b, 94t, 95b, 96t, 100t, 101b, 102, 104t, 105t, 107t, 112b, 113, 114t, 115t, 116t, /Museo Prenestino Palestrina 19t. **Bridgeman Art Library**: 14c, 29b, 33t, 46b, 53t, 57, 62t, 69, 75t, 120b, 124b, 125b. **Corbis**: 10t, 73b, 83, 84b, 88t, /Paul Almasy 4, 71t, /Archivo Iconografico 15c, 24b, 50b, 67t, 108t, 109t, 114b, 117, 120t, 123b, /Arte & Imagini srl, 109b, /Yann Arthus-Bertrand 115b, /Dave Bartruff 25t, /Bettmann 49b, 53b, 123t, /James P Blair 10b, /Jonathan Blair 88b, /Burstein Collection 46t, /Christie's Images 12r, 6–7, /Dean Conger 119, /Robert Estall 65b, /Macduff Everton 112t, /Jason Hawkes 125t, /John & Dallas Heaton 29t, /John Heseltine 22b, /Hulton – Deutsch 43b, /Hanan Isachar 121, /Mimmo Jodice 106t, /Araldo de Luca 16–17, 68t, 70b, Franz-Marc Frei 44b, /Francis G Mayer 12l, /Michael Nicholson 54t, /North Carolina Museum of Art 27t, /Richard T Nowitz 54b, /Dagli Orti 13l, 52b, /Carmen Redondo 35t, /Scheufler Collection 20b, /Stapleton Collection 74, /Liba Taylor 47t, /Gustavo Tomsich 23b, /Ruggero Vanni 35b, 72t, 98–9, /Vanni Archive 97b, 106b, /Sandro Vannini 48t, /Patrick Ward 116b, 124t, /Nik Wheeler 110–11, /Roger Wood 9, 11b, 89, 91t, 94b, /Adam Woolfitt 101t. **Dr Hazel Dodge**: 24t. **Mary Evans Picture Library**: 13c, 15r, 23t, 37. **Getty Images /Bridgeman**: 25b. **Robert Harding Picture Library**: 19b. **Scala, Florence**: 2–3, 8, 11t, 13r, 18b, 21, 22t, 26, 28, 30t, 31, 32, 34, 38–9, 40, 41t, 42t, 43t, 47b, 48b, 50t, 51t, 56, 63, 64, 65t, 66b, 67t, 68b, 71b, 76b, 77, 80–1, 84t, 86, 87t, 90, 91b, 92, 93, 95t, 96b, 100b, 104b, 105b, 107b, 108b, 118, 122.

ROME

TH RE

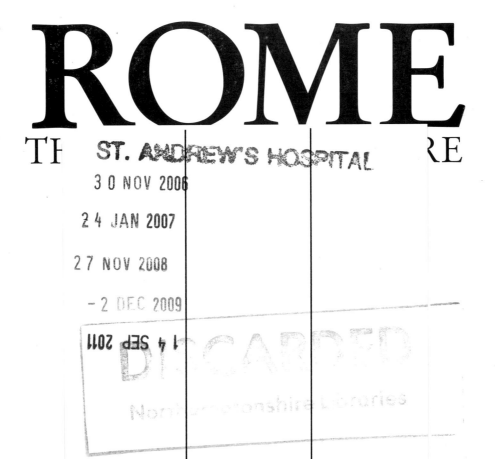

Please return/renew this item by the last
date shown. Books may also be renewed
by 'phone and the Internet

Northamptonshire Libraries and Information Service

 Northamptonshire
County Council

www.northamptonshire.gov.uk/leisure/libraries/

CONTENTS

ROME: THE WORLD'S FIRST SUPERPOWER 6
THE ARCHETYPAL EMPIRE 8
TIMELINE 12

ROME: THE WORLD'S FIRST SUPERPOWER

The rise of Rome, from the mythically simple beginnings of a few dwellings above the river Tiber to dominion over the whole Mediterranean world, was seen by Romans themselves as inevitable and divinely ordained. The qualities on which the Romans prided themselves – piety, fidelity and above all *virtus*, meaning courage, ability, strength and excellence – were what made their empire possible, indeed invincible. So long as its citizens retained them, Rome would remain mistress of the world. What is remarkable about Rome is that, almost without exception, it conquered all other powers, making it the sole superpower of the ancient Mediterranean world. This was a region where many of the great civilizations of antiquity – Egyptian, Babylonian, Carthaginian, Etruscan, Greek – converged, with only distant China ever rivalling Rome in stability, power and longevity. Rome was the heir of these ancient civilizations of the Middle East and Mediterranean, absorbing and propagating their cultures, while adding its own distinctive elements to make a civilization that was unique. When Rome finally fell, it not only left us its great architectural and engineering feats – aqueducts, arches, roads – but also the corpus of Roman law, the Catholic Church, and the idea of a universal empire that could extend its benefits to all under its sway, irrespective of racial background. Rome gave a huge area many centuries of peace, but it implanted also the ideal of a universal, basically benevolent state. This has made Rome an unrivalled cultural as well as political superpower, that continues to inspire and influence the world long after its fall.

Left: As Rome became the most wealthy and powerful city in the ancient world, it drew in foreigners as craftsmen, teachers, traders – and slaves.

THE ARCHETYPAL EMPIRE

Above: Rome's influence was as much cultural as political. The Deir, a temple-tomb at Petra, Jordan, was built in the 1st century AD in Roman-influenced style before Rome annexed Petra itself in AD106.

Below: The ceremonial Via Sacra (Sacred Way) runs through the Forum Romanum, which itself was the centre of Roman life. The Arch of Titus is visible in the background.

Rome remains the archetypal empire, the object of admiration, fascination and at times of repulsion. How a small settlement of farmers grew into an empire that ruled so much of the then known world is one of the greatest tales in history. The ruins left by Roman might – aqueducts, bridges, basilicas, arches, baths and temples, many still standing, a few still in use 2,000 years on – have cast a spell on subsequent generations. Rome's empire was not only large – it stretched from Scotland to Egypt – but it lasted a very long time. For six centuries, Rome was mistress of the Mediterranean and western Europe, its sphere of influence reaching even further. If Rome could fall, observers have wondered, how secure is our civilization? Greater than Rome's physical legacy, however, has been its influence on culture and institutions.

This book is written in the Roman (or Latin) alphabet. Nearly two-thirds of the words in the English language derive directly or indirectly from Latin, the Roman language. Spanish, French, Portuguese and Italian are Romance languages, direct descendants of Latin, originally the language of central Italy. The Senate, the upper house in countries like the United States and Ireland, is the Roman name for a Roman institution. The emblem of the United States and many now-vanished empires is an eagle, modelled on that of Jupiter, Rome's chief deity. The American motto, *E Pluribus Unum*, and the British motto, *Fidis Defensor*, are in Latin, the study of which was long considered essential for anybody with pretensions to education, and which is still useful for law and medicine.

Much of the world's law is derived from the legal codes of imperial Rome. The ideal of a world guided by common laws and international institutions, whether political, judicial or economic, owes much to Roman attempts, however imperfect, to create an empire based on law as much as force. The United States, the United Nations and the European Union – all implicitly reflect the influence of Roman universalism.

IMPERIALISM – HARD AND SOFT

Rome did not acquire or keep its empire by noble ideals or fine words. It was, first and last, a nation of soldiers. The triumphal arches the Romans erected around their empire celebrated bloody military victories. For a triumph, a general had to have killed at least 5,000 (sometimes 10,000) of the enemy. Our word emperor comes from *imperator*, victorious commander-in-chief, for emperors were above all the supreme generals of Rome.

As any of the peoples who revolted against Rome could attest, the Romans could be methodically brutal in their reprisals. Tacitus, greatest if gloomiest of Roman historians, has one Briton defeated by Rome's might say, "You made a desert and you called it peace." As Rome acquired its empire, it grew fantastically rich. By the 1st century AD, when Roman power was nearing its height, probably one person in three in the city of Rome was a slave. The whole Mediterranean world had to pay for the luxury and power of the conquerors, with money, goods and slaves. But if a few peoples rose in revolt, many others cooperated in what became a pan-imperial venture.

If Rome benefited from its empire – and empires are run, in the first instance, for the benefit of their rulers – then the advantages did not run all one way. As the empire matured, none of the privileges of being Roman was denied to former subject peoples. Rome was unique among ancient states in being ready to extend its citizenship to others. Under the empire, prosperity spread out in ripples, thanks to the benign aspects of Roman government. If people in the provinces paid taxes to Rome, these were often lighter than the taxes previously paid to their own rulers. In AD14, at the end of

his life, the first emperor Augustus was touched by a spontaneous demonstration. The passengers and crew of a ship just arrived from Alexandria put on garlands and burnt incense to him, saying they owed him their lives and liberty to sail the seas. These Alexandrians, from a great trading city but not Roman citizens, knew that their freedom and prosperity depended on the *Pax Romana*, the Roman peace that Augustus established and that his successors long maintained.

PAX ROMANA: THE ROMAN PEACE

It is easy to forget the benefits of external peace and internal security when they have become the accustomed way of life. Until well into the 19th century, however, most cities in continental Europe, like cities across Asia, were walled to protect them from attacks. What Rome gave the war-torn ancient world was unprecedented peace, security and stability for more than two centuries after Augustus reunited the empire in

Above: The empire in AD200, centred still on the Mediterranean, but now stretching from the Middle East to Scotland.

Below: The arch at Timgad, Algeria, commemorates Trajan, the city's founder. Cities were built across the empire with the full range of civic amenities: baths, theatres, amphitheatres, forums and triumphal arches.

Above: Rome's impact on Western culture has at times been almost overpowering. Pennsylvania Railroad Station in New York (built 1906–10, now demolished), simply recreated the interior of the huge baths of Caracalla in Rome, built 1700 years before.

Below: The Jefferson Memorial, Washington DC, repeats the form of the Pantheon in Rome of 1700 years earlier. This was a political and architectural homage, the young Republic saluting the ancient one.

30BC. Even the walls surrounding Rome were allowed to decay. Many cities across the empire also dispensed with walls, except for ceremonial perimeters. The Roman peace was upheld by a small army of some 300,000 men, perhaps half of one per cent of the population. The army itself was often occupied in building the network of *c.*50,000 miles (80,000km) of roads that stretched across the empire.

The Mediterranean Sea was cleared of pirates to become a marine highway dotted with seaside villas, a state of affairs not to recur until the 19th century. Land communications were better across Europe and western Asia under the Romans than at any other time until the coming of canals and railways. Lighthouses, from the great *pharos* of Alexandria in Egypt to many smaller examples, guided ships. With Rome's enduring peace, and its relatively light taxation, came novel prosperity. As city ruins show, some desert regions in north Africa and western Asia enjoyed under Roman rule a prosperity never to be repeated, while it took a millennium for most cities in western Europe to regain Roman levels of population and wealth.

MULTIRACIAL, MULTIFAITH

Much can be said against an empire that relied so heavily on slavery and a culture in which the chief entertainment of many citizens was watching men or animals fight one another, at times to death. But one accusation cannot be levelled against Rome: that of racism. When the Romans talked of "barbarians", the term simply denoted cultural and social backwardness and brutishness. The inhabitants of previously barbaric provinces, such as Gaul (France), North Africa and Spain, could and did become Romans, some eventually entering the Roman Senate – to the disgust of conservative senators. Several such "provincials" became emperors later in the empire. Racial background had no effect on a person's career. The emperor who presided over Rome's millennial jubilee in AD248 was called Philip the Arab because he came from Arabia Nabataea, now Jordan. Whole dynasties of emperors came from Libya, Spain and Syria. Rome extended the benefits of its empire ever wider, until finally in AD212 almost everyone except slaves acquired full Roman citizenship. Even slaves were being better treated by then, but slavery in a society with no colour bar was very different from that in 19th-century America. Many slaves were freed; a few prospered.

Romans, like most polytheists, were religiously tolerant. The myriad faiths of the empire were not suppressed but regulated, some being incorporated into the Roman pantheon. As long as subjects offered incense to the emperor – a political and not a religious gesture, as few educated Romans literally believed in the emperor's divinity – people had freedom of worship. The Roman suppression of Druidism in Britain, like the crushing of Jewish revolts in Judaea and later their intermittent persecutions of Christians, was political. The Druids potentially threatened Roman rule in Britain; the Jews had violently rejected Roman rule in Judaea and surrounding lands; and the Christians appeared to be disloyal.

Roman culture was so much influenced by the Greek that we often talk of "Graeco-Roman culture". This became effectively the cultural standard, even when influenced by local cultures – Roman civilization in Britain, for instance, was not identical to that in Syria. In the countryside especially, older beliefs and customs persisted beneath a Roman veneer. But it was possible to travel, unarmed, from Britain or Spain to Syria using one currency and speaking only two languages: Latin in the west and Balkans, Greek elsewhere. The traveller would have found that almost every city in the empire had its public baths, forum (market and meeting place), theatres, basilicas (halls), public games as well as students of Greek and Latin poetry and rhetoric. Rome conquered culturally as well as politically. Gauls, Spaniards, Africans and Britons adopted the Roman way of life as it seemed better than the alternatives. At the very least, this adoption helped the ambitious to rise.

ROME'S ENDURING LEGACY

The fall of the Roman empire in the west is irresistibly fascinating and rouses endless debate as to its causes. More significant is that the potent *idea* of the Roman empire did not expire in AD476. The Holy Roman Empire, created when Charlemagne was crowned by the Pope in Rome in AD800, attempted with some success to revive the empire, and it lasted for a millennium. Then Napoleon founded his short-lived empire, complete with eagles, triumphal arches and opportunities for other peoples to join the imperial regime. Perhaps, however, in the end the greatest heir of Rome was spiritual rather than military.

Within living memory, the Roman Catholic Church held all services in Latin, and the Pope still lives in Rome, in a line dating back almost 2000 years to St Peter, the first pope. As Eusebius, the "first Christian historian" (AD263–339), pointed out, it needed the peace and unity established by Augustus for Christianity to spread and establish itself. The Catholic

Church, with its hierarchy and its universalist ambitions, is the most obvious inheritor of ancient Rome.

Rome's greatest legacy is probably its universality, this longing to include all humanity within its realm. Rome's great poet Virgil voiced novel feelings for all human suffering. Rome's wars of conquest were often brutal, but the Roman peace atoned for this in the end. In the west especially, Roman culture went deep. Virgil's poetry was known to ordinary soldiers on Hadrian's Wall as evidence attests, not just to an elite.

> *"You created one homeland*
> *for the differing peoples*
> *Those without justice*
> *benefited from your rule;*
> *By allowing the vanquished*
> *to share in your own laws*
> *You made a city*
> *out of what was once the world."*

The words of the poet Namatianus, written around AD420, are poignant, as, only a few years earlier, the Goths had sacked Rome. His poem summarizes Rome's claim to be the universal city of humanity. To Rome as much as to Greece the world owes what has become Western civilization. The world without Rome would be unimaginably different. Arguably, it would be much the poorer.

Above: The Pantheon in Rome is among Rome's finest, best-preserved of temples, and its great dome has proved lastingly influential. It was built by the emperor Hadrian in AD118–28, but here it is shown as it was in the 18th century, with small towers.

Below: The Roman poet Virgil, flanked by two of the muses, was a protégé of the emperor Augustus. Virgil's greatest poem, the Aeneid, *became imperial Rome's epic, but it is an epic marked by concern for all humanity, not just the victors.*

TIMELINE

The history of Rome in its varying forms – as a tiny primitive kingdom, as an ever-growing republic, as a world-ruling empire and finally as the ghost or legend of that empire – stretches back to the early Iron Age. Its history really ends only in the 19th century, when the last Holy Roman Emperor abdicated and Napoleon Bonaparte crowned himself Emperor of the French in an obvious attempt to resurrect Rome's claims to universal empire.

The Romans themselves dated all events *ab urbe condita*, from the (mythical) foundation of the City by Romulus in 753BC – an event they saw, not without some reason, as being of world-transforming significance. Only in the 5th century AD did the present Christian calendar supersede the old Roman system.

Early dates down to at least 350BC remain very uncertain, but the broad sweep of Roman history remains unmistakeable and remarkable: the rise and ultimate fall of a mighty empire, whose memories lived on so potently that later rulers tried to resuscitate its titles and grandeurs.

Note: Very early dates, up to 350BC, are approximate.

753–451BC

753 Legendary founding of city by (mythical) brothers Romulus and Remus; Romulus reigns as sole king to 717, regarded by later Romans as actual founder of Rome.

*c.***650** The Etruscan kings (possibly Etruscan outcasts) arrive in Rome.

*c.***590** Solon reforms the Athenian constitution, making it semi-democratic.

578–535 Reign of Servius Tullius; forms the first Assembly, the *comitia centuriata*, on kinship lines.

534–509 Reign of Tarquinius Superbus, the last of the kings; building of first temple on Capitoline Hill.

509 Expulsion of Tarquin and end of Etruscan cultural predominance in Rome. Formation of Republic; kings replaced by elected officials, praetors and then consuls; first treaty with Carthage.

496 Rome defeats Latins at Battle of Lake Regillus; makes equal treaty of alliance with Latins.

494–440 Struggle of the Orders. Patricians (the 100 nobles supposedly chosen by Romulus) versus plebeians (everybody else).

493 First tribunes appointed to defend plebeian interests.

480 Greeks led by Athens defeat Persian invaders at Salamis; beginning of the classical age in Greece.

474 Battle of Cumae: Greeks defeat Etruscans and Carthaginians at sea; beginnings of Etruscan decline.

471 Creation of new Assembly of the Plebs, which elects tribunes annually.

450–300BC

450 Twelve Tables of the Law published; the first written laws help plebeians.

449 Tribunes increased to ten and their sacrosanctity legally guaranteed.

440 *Lex Cannuleia* establishes equality between plebs and patricians; institution of censors.

431–404 Peloponnesian War between Athens and Sparta; Athens defeated.

425 Fidenae (city) taken from Veii.

421 First plebeian quaestor.

405–396 Long siege and capture of Veii, the key to southern Etruria.

*c.***400** Celts (Gauls) invade northern Italy.

*c.***390** Sack of Rome by invading Gauls.

386 Rome grants citizens of Caere *hospitium publicum*, privileged status.

*c.***378** Building of Servian wall.

367 One consul must always be plebeian.

343–41 First war against Samnites, highland people.

338 Defeat of the Latins; Latin League dissolved; Roman power extends into Campania.

336–323 Alexander the Great of Macedon overwhelms Greek states and conquers Persian empire before dying in Babylon. His empire is divided between his generals, the Diadochi (successors).

329 Terracina becomes a Roman colony.

327–304 Second Samnite War.

321 Romans defeated by Samnites at Caudine Forks.

312 Censorship of Appius Claudius; building of first Roman road, the Via Appia to Capua, and Aqua Appia, Rome's first aqueduct.

299–200BC

298–90 Third Samnite War.

295 Samnites defeated at Sentium.

287 *Lex Hortensia*: plebiscites (votes of the people) become law.

280–275 War with King Pyrrhus of Epirus.

275 Romans defeat Pyrrhus.

264–241 First Punic War.

260 Romans build their first fleet.

259 Roman victory at sea at Mylae.

256–55 Regulus invades Africa, but is defeated.

249 Romans defeated at Drapana.

241 Final Roman victory off the Aègates Islands; Sicily the first Roman province.

238 Sardinia and Corsica annexed.

223 Successful Roman campaigns in Cisalpine Gaul lead to first colonies there.

220 Censorship of Flaminius; builds Via Flaminia to Rimini and Circus Flaminius.

219 Hannibal besieges and takes Saguntum in Spain.

218–202 Second Punic War.

218–217 Hannibal crosses Alps; his army defeats Romans at Ticinus and later at Trebbia.

216 Roman defeat at Cannae; Hannibal forms alliance with Philip V of Macedonia; some allies abandon Rome.

214–205 First Macedonian War.

213–211 Siege of Syracuse.

211–206 Scipio campaigns in Spain.

209 Scipio captures Cartagena.

207 Hasdrubal leads army into Italy.

203 Scipio invades Africa, wins Battle of the Great Plains.

202 Scipio defeats Hannibal at Zama. End of Carthaginian overseas power.

199–100BC

200–196 Second Macedonian War.

197–179 Gracchus ends wars in Spain; Spain organized into two provinces.

197 Philip V of Macedon defeated.

196 Flaminius declares "freedom of the Greeks" at Isthmia, near Corinth.

194 Romans evacuate Greece.

191 Cisalpine Gaul (northern Italy) conquered by Rome.

190 Seleucid king Antiochus III of Syria defeated at Magnesia; Seleucids expelled from Asia Minor.

184 Censorship of Cato the Elder.

179 Aemilian bridge, first stone bridge over Tiber, built.

168 Perseus of Macedonia defeated at Pydna; Macedonia becomes Roman dependency.

167 Direct taxation of Roman citizens abolished; sack of Epirus, 150,000 Greeks enslaved; Jewish revolt led by Maccabeus against Antiochus IV; Polybius arrives in Rome as hostage.

149–146 Third Punic War; Africa (northern Tunisia) becomes Roman province.

146 Corinth and Carthage sacked, Achaea and Macedonia Roman provinces.

141 Parthians capture Babylon: final decline of Seleucid empire.

136–32 First Sicilian Slave War.

133 Tiberius Gracchus killed; kingdom of Pergamum (western Asia Minor) left to Rome by last king.

107–100 Marius consul six times; reforms army, defeats Cimbri and Teutones and Jugurtha of Numidia (Algeria).

103–100 Second Sicilian Slave War.

99–1BC

91 Beginning of Social War.

90 *Lex Julia*: full citizenship for Italians.

89–85 First war against Mithradates.

87 Marius seizes power in Rome.

86 Sulla sacks Athens.

82 Sulla becomes dictator; second Mithradatic War.

80 Sulla resigns dictatorship.

73–71 Slave revolt of Spartacus.

70 Consulship of Pompey and Crassus.

67 Pompey eliminates pirates.

66 Pompey given eastern command.

63 Consulship of Cicero.

60 First Triumvirate: Pompey, Crassus and Caesar.

59 Caesar consul for the first time.

58–51 Caesar's Gallic Wars.

55–54 Caesar "invades" Britain.

53 Crassus killed at Carrhae.

49 Caesar crosses the Rubicon.

48 Pompey defeated at Pharsalus; Caesar meets Cleopatra, and they become lovers.

44 Caesar assassinated.

43 Second Triumvirate: Antony, Octavian and Lepidus. Murder of Cicero.

42 Republicans defeated at Philippi: empire divided.

36 Octavian defeats Sextus Pompeius.

31 Battle of Actium.

30 Suicides of Antony and Cleopatra; Egypt annexed by Octavian; Roman empire reunited.

27 Octavian assumes title *Augustus*.

16–9 Annexations of Alpine and Balkan regions under Tiberius; Drusus reaches the Elbe.

12 Death of Agrippa.

AD1–49

4 Death of Gaius forces Augustus to recall Tiberius from exile in Rhodes.

6 Judaea becomes Roman province after death of Herod the Great (in 4BC); start of the Great Pannonian revolt (lasting until AD9), which distracts Tiberius from planned campaigns in Germany.

8 Poet Ovid exiled to Tomis on Black Sea.

9 Disastrous loss of three legions in Germany under Varus; frontier withdrawn to Rhine.

14 Death of Augustus; Tiberius succeeds as emperor; Germanicus quashes Rhine legions' mutiny and campaigns into Germany to avenge Varus' defeat.

19 Death of Germanicus, the designated heir, in Syria.

27 Tiberius retires to villa on Capri, fuelling rumours of his depravities there; Sejanus acts as his sole minister in Rome.

30 or 33 Crucifixion of Jesus.

31 Execution of Sejanus for conspiracy.

37 Death of Tiberius; accession of Gaius Caligula; birth of Nero.

41 Assassination of Caligula; Claudius succeeds him as emperor. Annexation of Mauretania (Algeria/Morocco) as two imperial provinces.

42 Abortive rebellion of Scribonus, governor of Dalmatia.

43 Invasion of Britain, which becomes province. Claudius increasingly relies on freedmen, who form the nucleus of imperial civil service.

46 Thrace becomes province.

49 Claudius marries his niece Agrippina; Seneca becomes Nero's tutor.

AD50–99

51 Caratacus, British prince, defeated and captured.

54 Death of Claudius; accession of Nero; Seneca and Burrus joint chief ministers.

59 Murder of Agrippina, Nero's over-powering mother.

60–1 Revolt of Boudicca and the Iceni in Britain; sack of London, Colchester and St Albans.

62 Death of Burrus and end of Seneca's influence; Nero increasingly extravagant

63–6 Settlement of Armenia and eastern frontier by Corbulo.

64 Great Fire of Rome; Nero persecutes Christians as scapegoats. Begins building the Golden House.

66–70 First Jewish War; Vespasian and Titus suppress Jewish revolt.

68 Suicide of Nero; accession of Galba.

68–9 Year of the Four Emperors: Galba, then Vitellius proclaimed emperor, then Otho, who commits suicide, leaving Vespasian sole emperor.

70 Capture and sack of Jerusalem.

79 Death of Vespasian; accession of Titus; destruction of Pompeii and Herculaneum by Vesuvius.

80 Inauguration of Colosseum at Rome.

81 Death of Titus; accession of Domitian.

85–92 Dacians check Domitian's campaigns and force subsidy payment.

88 Start of construction of *limes*, patrolled frontiers, along the line of the Neckar to cut off the Rhine-Danube re-entrant angle.

96 Assassination of Domitian; Nerva proclaimed emperor by Senate.

98 Death of Nerva; accession of Trajan.

AD100–199

101–6 Trajan's campaigns lead to new province of Dacia (Romania).

106 Annexation of Arabia Petraea (Jordan).

111–14 Construction of Trajan's column and forum at Rome; they are dedicated in 112–13.

113–17 War with Parthians. Conquest of Armenia, Assyria and Mesopotamia (Iraq).

115–17 Jewish revolt in Cyprus, Cyrene and Egypt.

117 Death of Trajan; accession of Hadrian.

118–28 Building of Pantheon, Rome.

121–2 Hadrian visits Britain; starts building of Hadrian's Wall.

131–5 Jewish revolt under Bar Kochba defeated; Jerusalem left a ruin.

138 Death of Hadrian; accession of Antoninus Pius.

142 Building of Antonine Wall across Scotland; Hadrian's Wall abandoned.

150–63 Revolt in northern Britain and abandonment of Antonine Wall.

161 Death of Antoninus; accession of Marcus Aurelius and Lucius Verus.

162–6 Parthian War. Ctesiphon and Seleucia sacked; plague brought back.

167 Marcomanni and Quadi, Germanic tribes, raid across Danube and reach Italy.

168–80 Wars of Marcus Aurelius.

180 Death of Marcus; accession of Commodus; peace with the Germans.

192 Commodus murdered; civil war.

193 Septimius Severus emperor in Rome.

195–9 Severus' Parthian campaigns.

AD200–299

211 Severus dies in York; leaves empire to sons Caracalla and Geta. Caracalla murders Geta.

212 *Constitutio Antoniniana*: Roman citizenship for all free men in empire.

217 Assassination of Caracalla, briefly succeeded by Macrinus.

218 Accession of Elagabalus.

222 Assassination of Elagabalus; accession of Alexander Severus; effective rule of Julia Mamaea, his mother.

235 Assassination of Alexander Severus; anarchy for almost 50 years – at least 30 emperors.

241 Shapur I (to 272), new Persian king, determined to revive old Persian empire.

251 Emperor Decius killed by Goths; plague ravages empire; persecution of Christians.

253–60 Valerian and Gallienus become co-emperors; Persian invasions.

260 "Gallic empire" formed. Valerian captured by Persians; sole reign of Gallienus; army reorganized, adminstrative capital moved to Milan.

268 Zenobia, Queen of Palmyra, breaks away with eastern provinces and Egypt.

270 Accession of Aurelian.

273 Zenobia defeated by Aurelian.

284 Accession of Diocletian; joint rule with Maximian as Augusti in 286.

286–96 Breakaway British "empire" under Carausius and Allectus.

293 Constantius I and Galerius appointed Caesars in new tetrarchy.

297–8 Persian War brings new Roman gains in east (now Kurdistan).

AD300–399

303–11 Last persecution of Christians.

305 Diocletian and Maximian retire.

306 Death of Constantius; his son Constantine I acclaimed emperor by troops but recognized only as Caesar of western provinces by other rulers.

312 Maxentius defeated at Milvian Bridge; Constantine sole ruler in west.

313 Edict of Milan: religious tolerance.

324 Constantine becomes sole emperor.

324–30 Foundation of Constantinople as New Rome.

325 Church Council of Nicaea presided over by Constantine.

337 Death of Constantine; empire split between his three sons: Constantine II (d. 340), Constantius II (d. 361) and Constans (d. 350).

355 Julian appointed Caesar in west.

361–3 Sole reign of Julian, pagan restoration; killed on Persian campaign.

364 Valens and Valentinian I joint emperors.

375 Valentinian dies of stroke.

378 Valens killed by invading Goths at battle of Adrianople; Goths occupy Roman territory south of Danube.

379 Theodosius I becomes emperor; accepts the Goths as federates.

382 Removal of Altar of Victory from Senate House; campaign against pagans.

394 Battle of the Cold River; Theodosius defeats rivals Argobast and Eugenius.

395 On his death, Theodosius divides empire between sons: Honorius emperor in west, Arcadius in east. Stilicho effective ruler in west.

AD400–535

404 Western imperial court moved from Milan to Ravenna, secure behind marshes.

406 German invaders cross frozen Rhine and sack Trier, the Gallic capital.

410 Last troops withdrawn from Britain; Visigoths under Alaric sack Rome; Alaric dies; Goths later settle in southwest Gaul.

421 Constantine III becomes effective ruler of western empire.

425 Valentinian III emperor in west; mother Galla Placidia at first is real ruler.

434 Attila becomes king of the Huns.

439 Vandals capture Carthage.

446 "Groans of the Britons": traditional last appeal by Romanized Britons for imperial help.

451 Battle of Châlons: Huns defeated by joint forces of Visigoths and Romans under Aetius.

452 Attila's invasion of Italy halted by Pope Leo I.

454 Murder of Aetius.

455 Death of Valentinian III; Vandals sack Rome.

476 Last emperor Romulus Augustulus deposed by mercenary chief Odoacer, who takes power himself. End of the western empire; imperial insignia sent to Constantinople.

493 Theodoric, king of Ostrogoths, becomes ruler of Italy.

527 Accession of Justinian I as emperor in Constantinople.

533 Belisarius, Byzantine general, reconquers North Africa from Vandals.

535 Belisarius begins reconquest of Italy.

CHAPTER I

AN EMPIRE OF FORCE AND LAW

Rome did not acquire its empire in a few dazzling victories, but piecemeal, sometimes unintentionally, if very rarely peacefully. Rome's growth from a small settlement on the Tiber into a great empire was largely due to its military prowess and ruthless aggressiveness. Military service was a central part of life for Roman citizens. Adaptable, superbly disciplined and incredibly tough, the Roman army made Rome an imperial power. This gradual and methodical process took many hundreds of years. While such an approach may have lacked glamour, it certainly created an empire that proved very long-lived.

If most Romans experienced army life, many were also lawyers. Roman respect for the law and legality, although there was no written constitution, long safeguarded the civilian basis of politics. For a surprisingly long time, the Roman army did not intervene in civilian affairs. Its generals, no matter how great their victories, had to relinquish their commands as they entered the city, becoming ordinary citizens again and liable to prosecution for any misconduct. Even the emperor did not claim to be above the law and wore a toga (civilian dress), not armour. Rome also freely extended its citizenship to ever more cities, one of the main secrets of its success as an imperial power.

Left: This detail from the Arch of Constantine in Rome shows Emperor Constantine addressing his army – the sometimes rebellious basis of Rome's imperial might.

LEGENDARY BEGINNINGS
753–509BC

Above: Controlling the lowest crossing of the river Tiber, Rome was poised to dominate the valley of central Italy's largest river when it gained the power to do so. For long periods, however, the Tiber was as much a boundary as a route for expansion inland.

According to legend Rome was founded in 753BC by Romulus and Remus, twin princes of Alba Longa, supposedly itself founded four centuries earlier by Aeneas, a Trojan prince. The twins, his distant descendants, were abandoned as babies on the orders of Amulius, who had usurped their kingdom and ordered their deaths. Miraculously, a she-wolf appeared from a wood to suckle them, and they were brought up by Faustinus, a kindly shepherd, on the Palatine Hill. When they grew up, they killed the usurper and together founded a new city: Rome. But they soon quarrelled, Romulus killing Remus for jumping over his ploughed boundary line. Romulus then populated Rome by inviting outlaws and homeless men to join him, and by abducting the young women of his neighbours in the famous "Rape of the Sabine Women". When the Sabine men marched back in force to reclaim their women, the latter, by now used to being Roman wives, intervened to prevent a battle and the two peoples intermarried. Romulus later ascended into heaven in a thunderstorm, becoming divine. From such violent, mythic beginnings sprang the Eternal City, Rome.

THE EARLY SETTLEMENTS

Archaeology tells us that by the mid-8th century BC an unimpressive settlement existed on the Palatine Hill. The first Romans were actually Latin farmers or shepherds, the Latins being a subgroup of the Italian peoples, living in separate villages of small huts on the Palatine and the Esquiline Hills. Beneath and between these hills were marshy valleys. Despite later Roman propaganda to the contrary, this was not a particularly healthy or fertile spot, but an island had two advantages. In the midst of the fast-flowing river Tiber, it offered the first practical crossing upriver from the sea 16 miles (25km) distant, while the hills provided good defensive positions.

The settlements remained extremely primitive until the arrival – once again enshrined in myth – of the Etruscan Kings, who traditionally ruled Rome from 616 to 509BC. Certainly, at about this time Rome came under the sway of the Etruscans. They were a civilized people who dominated Italy from Bologna to the Bay of Naples. Rome's strategic position on the Tiber meant the Etruscans, approaching the height of their power, inevitably wanted control over it. In close contact with the Greek cities to the south, whose art influenced but did not overwhelm their art, the Etruscans were a cheerful, even hedonistic, race, fond of the arts, women, banquets and athletics – or so their surviving bronzes and tomb paintings suggest. We still cannot fully read their language, even though, like the Roman alphabet, it uses a version of the Greek alphabet, but the Etruscans did not write very much.

Right: According to legend, the twins Romulus and Remus, distant descendants of the Trojan prince Aeneas, were suckled by a she-wolf after they had been abandoned as babies. In 753BC they founded the city of Rome, which bears Romulus' name.

A NEW CITY

It is probably true to say that the kings made Rome a city rather than a mere huddle of villages. The *Forum Romanum*, the market/meeting place, heart of the city and later of the empire, was established on drained marshland and paved, as was the *Forum Boarium* (cattle market) close to the river.

Tarquinius Priscus, the "good Tarquin", who ruled between *c.*616 and 579BC, held the first census. Citizens were organized into three tribes, each having ten *curiae*, or wards. From these 30 wards the kings chose 300 patricians, or heads of extended families, to sit in the advisory council known as the Senate. The first Assembly, the *comitia curiata*, is also thought to have emerged about this time, although its powers are unknown.

Priscus' successor, King Servius Tullius, reorganized the state, dividing Romans into five classes according to their wealth. Each class was subdivided into centuries, each century being roughly equal in wealth. All citizens were liable for army service, apart from those in the last and poorest class, who could not afford to arm themselves. A legion, or levy, had 6,000 infantry and 300 cavalry, the cavalry being provided by the richest century. In the newly appointed *comitia centuriata*, or Assembly by Hundreds, each century voted as a single block, with the richest (but smallest) century voting first. The vote was decided as soon as an absolute majority of centuries was reached, which inevitably gave the rich centuries the most influence and the poorest (and biggest) centuries the least. Rome never operated on the principle of "one man one vote".

At this time Rome acquired Ostia at the mouth of the Tiber as well as its first wooden bridge across the river. The period culminated in the construction of the first temple to Jupiter, king of the gods, on the Capitoline Hill. Originally simply constructed, the temple was later rebuilt ever more splendidly, and became *the* symbol of Roman power.

Above: The first Romans lived in simple huts, as shown in this mosaic of life on the Nile.

THE FOUNDING OF THE REPUBLIC

Around 509BC, the kings were suddenly and finally expelled, and the word Etruscan, like the word king, became an insult among Romans. According to legend, the last Etruscan king, Tarquinius Superbus, meaning "the proud", so angered the Roman nobles that they drove him out and declared a Republic, which they dominated through the Senate. From now on, the state was to be run by annually elected officials A new regime based on puritanical, patriotic *virtus*, or courage, was established that would serve Rome well through its coming struggles.

Below: This landscape is typical of the often wild mountains of central Italy east of Rome.

THE CONQUEST OF ITALY
501–266BC

Above: Rome alternately fought and treated with its often powerful Etruscan neighbours. This fresco from the 3rd century BC shows a treaty being agreed.

Below: The Via Appia, the first great Roman road, was built to connect Rome with Capua in 312BC and was later extended to Brindisi.

After the expulsion of the Etruscan kings Rome became less wealthy and powerful. The other cities of Latium, which were similar in language (Latin) and culture to Rome, turned against her. Surrounded by enemies, especially the Samnites to the east and the Volscians to the south, Rome was forced to ally itself with them on equal terms – although it was never to accept equality with any city for long.

THE RISE OF THE PLEBEIANS
Inside Rome, the advent of the Republic caused an economic slump. This triggered a lengthy conflict, which was known as the Conflict of the Orders or classes, between the people (plebeians) and the patricians, the old heads of the family who traced their descent from the original Senate members and who still monopolized power. In 494BC the plebeians – who included some moderately rich citizens and many independent farmers or artisans – threatened to secede from the state and leave Rome. These people formed the core of the army, so it was a very serious threat. After several attempts, the plebeians' threat worked and they acquired two tribunes of the people, special officials to defend their interests. Later, in 449BC, their number was increased to ten and they were given special status, regarded as sacrosanct or defended by the gods.

In 471BC the tribunes summoned a special Assembly of the Plebs to run alongside existing councils. At this time, only patricians could interpret the unwritten laws. Only in 450BC were laws written down on 12 tables of stone for everyone to see. These tables, often masterpieces of legal precision, became the foundation of Roman justice. In 421BC the first plebeian quaestors were elected, and from 367BC one of the two consuls (the top magistrates who led the armies) had to be a plebeian. The patricians tried to transfer some of the consul's powers to a new official, the quaestor, but from 337BC there was also a plebeian praetor. Finally, in 287BC a law, the Lex Hortensia (Roman laws were named after their proposer), declared that plebiscites, votes of the plebeian Assembly, could become law. This completed a social revolution without bloodshed – albeit with much dispute – and is an example of the Roman genius for pragmatism.

EXPANSION AND INVASION
Throughout this domestic turmoil, Rome steadily expanded its influence and territory. To the north, just across the Tiber, stood the wealthy Etruscan city of Veii, controlling a network of roads. Rome became involved in an intermittent 40-year war with this great rival. It ended only after Camillus, made emergency ruler, forced the army to campaign continuously – without even stopping for the harvest – and used a drainage tunnel to capture Veii in

Left: Paestum was one of the first Greek cities in southern Italy to be conquered by Rome in the 4th century BC. Its magnificent temple of Ceres, with massive Doric columns, is one of the best-preserved of the early Greek temples and dates from c.500BC.

396BC. This was a very important conquest. Overnight, it almost doubled Rome's territory, and the way to Etruria (Tuscany/Umbria) was opened.

A few years later, however, Rome faced acute danger. A horde of Gauls, barbarous Celts, swept through Italy in 390BC. Rome sent the whole of its army – some 15,000 men – to face them, but the Gauls, twice that number and better fighters, destroyed it almost completely. The city lay defenceless and most Romans fled, apart from a garrison on Capitoline Hill and some elderly senators who, as Livy related, "went home to await the enemy, fearless". A general massacre ensued and Rome was burnt to the ground.

MASTERING PENINSULAR ITALY
After this disaster many were tempted to abandon Rome, but Camillus rallied them to rebuild the city. In 378BC the Servian wall was constructed. It was 12ft (3.6m) thick and 24ft (7.5m) high and enclosed 1,000 acres (427 ha) – then a huge area. Rome would not fall to barbarians again for 800 years. Troubles with Rome's Latin allies followed, however. After peaceful methods of dealing with them failed, a four-year period of dogged fighting ensued before the Romans gained final victory in 338BC. The Latin League was dissolved, with each city being linked to Rome while retaining internal autonomy. Many were given citizenship, without voting rights (*civitas sine suffragio*). This halfway status satisfied the Latin cities and was a stroke of political genius. Another series of wars against the Samnites lasted nearly 40 years, with Rome suffering a major defeat in 321BC. But again Rome rallied, the Latin cities remained loyal and the first great Roman road, the Via Appia, was constructed to supply the army in the south. The war ended in 290BC with Rome undisputed mistress of central Italy.

Rome now came into contact with the Greek cities of southern Italy. A dispute with the largest, Tarento, led to war in 280BC. The Tarentines hired King Pyrrhus of Epirus, a renowned Greek mercenary leader. Pyrrhus' army included war elephants, the first seen in Italy, and he defeated the Romans twice, marching right into Latium. But Rome adapted its infantry tactics to cope with the elephants and crack Greek spearmen. By 272BC Pyrrhus had left Italy, and Tarento and the other Greek cities accepted Roman alliance. Throughout peninsular Italy, Rome was supreme.

Above: After the Gauls sacked Rome in 390BC, the Romans built the great Servian Wall some 24ft (7.5m) high. When it was completed in 378BC, the wall made the city all but impregnable to later attacks.

THE GROWTH OF EMPIRE
264–133BC

Above: The Carthaginians regularly used elephants, the "tanks of ancient warfare", in battle. The Roman legionaries soon learnt how to counter them, however, and they did not much affect the Punic wars.

Below: Lake Trasimene in Umbria was the scene of one of Rome's great defeats by Hannibal's armies in 217BC. The Carthaginians trapped the Romans by the lakeside and drove them into the water.

Facing each other across the Messina straits, Rome and Carthage had friendly treaties dating back to 509BC. But tensions soon developed between these two great powers of the western Mediterranean. Founded in *c.*800BC by Phoenician (Lebanese) traders, Carthage had extended its power along the African coast to Tangier and into Spain, founding Malaga and Cadiz. It also had control of most of Sicily. Larger and far richer than Rome, Carthage was ruled by a mercantile oligarchy whose faults showed up Rome's virtues. It relied on mercenary armies whom it often did not pay, led by Carthaginian generals whom it failed to support in success but always punished in defeat. However, as a city of merchants it had an excellent navy, while Rome, a land power, had no navy at all.

The clash came in 264BC when Messina appealed for Roman help against Carthage. Unusually, the Senate let the Assembly decide the issue. The Roman people voted for war and the first of three Punic Wars (the Roman name for Carthaginians) began. Lacking a fleet, Rome decided to build one, copying a captured Carthaginian ship, but adding a new weapon: the *corvus*, or raven, a bridge fitted with spikes that crashed down and stuck on to enemy vessels. This allowed Roman soldiers to board the enemy ship and fight as if on land. With this weapon a sea battle was won off Mylae in 259BC, but the war turned against Rome when it sent an army to Africa under Regulus. After initial victories, he was crushingly defeated in 255BC and a relief fleet was lost in a storm. At immense cost the Romans built another fleet, and finally in 241BC routed the Carthaginians off the Agate Islands. In its defeat, Carthage was forced to abandon Sicily, which became the first Roman *provincia*, or imperial possession, apart from the great city of Syracuse. This became Rome's first client kingdom or protectorate. Rome had won by tenacity, adaptability and the loyalty of the Italian allies, who supplied Rome's armies with fresh recruits to replace those killed in battle.

A WAR OF ATTRITION

Carthage, plunged into chaos by a revolt of its unpaid mercenaries, stood by as Rome annexed Sardinia and Corsica, the former long a Punic possession. However, Hamilcar Barca, a Carthaginian general, carved out new territory in Spain, where he recruited a better army financed by Spain's silver mines. His son Hannibal took command in 221BC, determined to strike directly at Italy, the source of Rome's vast military manpower. In 218BC Hannibal marched his army, including 37 elephants, over the Alps in a snowstorm. Hannibal's skills, combined with Roman amateurishness, led to a series of Carthaginian victories, leaving Rome almost defenceless after the third annihilating defeat at Cannae in 216BC. Amazingly, only a few allied cities –

Capua, Tarento, Syracuse – changed sides, and Hannibal could not capture Rome itself, although he rode around its walls. With cool courage, the Senate then sent an army to Spain to strike at Hannibal's base. After some initial defeats, Cornelius Scipio landed in 210BC, and in 206 ousted the Carthaginians. Spain now became a Roman possession, divided into two provinces. Meanwhile, in Italy, the Romans had adopted the "scorched earth" policy of Fabius *Cunctator*, the Delayer. This denied Hannibal all resources, but also devastated Italian farms and caused massive homelessness. The war of attrition ended in 204BC when Scipio landed in Africa, and Carthage, which had seldom reinforced Hannibal, recalled its general. At the battle of Zama in 202BC Hannibal was defeated by Scipio, and Carthage accepted a humiliating peace.

ROME AND THE EAST

The Second Punic War was the most momentous in Rome's history. It determined that Rome would rule the western Mediterranean and be arbiter in the east. Rome had already been drawn east, for Philip V of Macedonia (northern Greece) had allied with Carthage in 214BC, when Rome seemed doomed. This First Macedonian War petered out in 205BC but five years later, fearing that Philip was growing too powerful, Rome intervened more decisively, defeating him in 197BC. The Roman general Flaminius then promised "the liberty of the Greeks", meaning self-rule, to the feuding southern Greek cities. Antiochus III, the Seleucid (Hellenistic) king (one of Alexander the Great's successors), was decisively defeated in 190BC when he tried to intervene in Greece, his pan-Asian empire reduced to a Syrian rump. Rome then established a free port at Delos, which soon became the commercial centre of the eastern Mediterranean, thronged with Italian merchants, and a centre of the booming slave trade. Rome defeated Macedonia again in 168BC when it tried to reassert itself, finally

making all Macedonia a province in 146BC along with Greece itself. When the last ruler of Pergamum, another wealthy Hellenistic kingdom in Asia Minor, died in 133BC, he bequeathed it to Rome.

A NEW IMPERIALISM

The sack of Corinth, Greece's richest port, in 146BC, revealed a new brutality and rapacity in Roman imperialism. Although the Senate enjoyed prestige and power both at home and abroad, it did not always act wisely. The final destruction of Carthage in the Third Punic War was partly due to Cato the Censor, a reactionary who ended every speech with "Carthage must be destroyed!" But it was also due to Rome's increasingly aggressive imperialism. Vast fortunes were being made by Roman nobles who returned from military triumphs, or even from provincial governorships, with huge amounts of booty, including slaves. The destruction of Epirus in 167BC brought in 150,000 Greek slaves alone. Very often these captives were better educated than their masters and helped introduce Greek culture to Roman society. However, the gains of war came at a cost. The stability of the Republic was threatened by the plight of tens of thousands of impoverished Romans, forced off the land during the Punic Wars and now unemployed in Rome.

Above: The meeting of the Roman general Scipio and his opponent Hannibal just before the Battle of Zama in 202BC is one of the most famous encounters in history. Scipio crushed Hannibal's army the following day.

Below: By the 2nd century BC Rome was developing its own distinctive architecture, shown here in the Temple of Portunus. Although influenced by Greek precursors, its layout was uniquely Roman.

VICTORY ABROAD, DISCORD AT HOME: 133–61BC

Above: Vital in transporting troops and goods, the Romans invested time, effort and money in developing a good road system. This is a view of the Via Appia to the south of Rome.

Below: A great soldier and military reformer, Marius was also very much a man of the people, often re-elected consul against the Senate's wishes. As a politician, however, he proved disastrously inept.

The problems of small farmers, the backbone of Rome's citizen army, became acute in the 130sBC. During the Second Punic War, many had been forced to abandon their farms. Unable to regain them when they came home, the farmers sold out to larger landowners and many migrated to Rome in search of work. But Rome had no industry and soon many farmers fell into the poorest class, thereby becoming ineligible for military service. This hardly worried the Roman oligarchy, itself growing ever richer.

AGRARIAN REFORM

In 133BC Tiberius Gracchus was elected tribune. A member of the aristocracy but schooled in Greek philosophy, Tiberius proposed that *ager publicus*, public land, often gained by conquest but which the rich had grabbed, should be redistributed to the poor in small lots. Such a proposal was half-expected, but what alarmed the Senate was that Tiberius proposed his reform directly to the Assembly, without taking it through the Senate, employing the *Lex Hortensia* to start a land commission. He then flouted custom by trying to have himself re-elected tribune. Tiberius also issued a challenge to the Senate's power over foreign policy. It was this, perhaps even more than his land reforms, that so enraged conservative senators, who mobilized their supporters and had Tiberius and 300 of his followers clubbed to death. Blood had been shed in Roman politics for the first time in nearly four centuries.

Ten years later Gaius, the more radical younger brother of Tiberius, re-enacted the agrarian reforms and proposed establishing colonies of landless citizens at recently conquered Carthage while subsidizing grain for the poor. To pay for this, he auctioned the rights to collect taxes in the new province of Asia to the knights (equestrians), to whom he also transferred control of the criminal law courts from the Senate. This boosted the knightly, or equestrian, order, the second richest class, which in turn increasingly challenged the Senate's powers. Gaius, too, paid for his reforms with his life. He failed to be elected for a third time as tribune and was killed as the Senate issued a *senatus consultum ultimum*, or Senate's final decree. From now on the Senate would be divided between the optimates, in reality reactionaries, and the *populares*, nobles and others who took the people's side or more often utilized popular support for their own ends. The struggle between these two factions in the end wrecked the Republic.

MARIUS AND SULLA

Rome's growing military weakness was starkly exposed by defeats in Mauretania (western North Africa), whose king Jugurtha proved invincible until the election of Gaius Marius as consul. Marius did not come from the nobility, and his frequent re-election as consul – seven times in all – revealed the new powers of the Assembly. Realizing that the legions badly needed recruits from proletarians, the landless citizens, Marius abolished all property qualifications for the army, while making it semi-professional with proper equipment. He encouraged legionaries to look to their generals, not the Senate, for rewards after service. This tie between general and army was fatally to undermine the Republic.

At first, Marius seemed the Republic's saviour. With his revitalized army he crushed the Cimbri and Teutones – barbarians who had overwhelmed two Roman armies – at Aix-en-Provence and in the Po valley in 102–1BC. The Senate then had to accept proposals that Marius'

Left: The Aegean island of Delos benefited from the Roman conquest, which made it a free port. Soon it was the most thriving port in the Mediterranean and a centre of the booming slave trade, until it was sacked by Mithradates' Greek allies in 88BC.

POMPEY AND CRASSUS

Spartacus, a gladiator, started a slave revolt at Capua in 73BC that spread throughout southern Italy. Crassus, notorious for his wealth, organized an army to suppress it, helped in the last stages by Pompey, once Sulla's youngest lieutenant. With their armies backing them, the two men became consuls in 70BC, and undid Sulla's measures, restoring the courts to the knights and reducing the Senate's powers. The problem of pirates threatening Rome's corn supply then became pressing, but Pompey, given overall command by the *Lex Gabinia* in 67BC, swept the Mediterranean clear of pirates in three months. His command was extended over the whole east, which he reorganized from the Caspian to the Red Sea. Returning home in 62BC, he disbanded his army but was annoyed at being denied his expected triumph by the Senate. He then formed the First Triumvirate, or Gang of Three, with Crassus and Julius Caesar, a rising *popularis* leader. From this moment, the days of the Republic were numbered.

veterans be given lands in Gaul, Greece and Africa as rewards when Marius marched south with some troops. In 90BC the Italian allies, who had been promised but had never received full citizenship, rose in revolt across Italy. The ensuing war was chiefly won by the *Lex Julia*, granting all free men south of the Po Roman citizenship. The war left more farmers uprooted and more ex-soldiers looking for rewards.

Lucius Cornelius Sulla, one of Marius' ablest generals but a die-hard optimate, went east in 86BC to defeat Mithradates, king of Pontus, who had invaded Greece. Meanwhile Marius, elected consul for the last time, massacred opponents with his troops before dying in January 87BC. The *populares'* triumph was brief. In 82BC Sulla returned from the east without disbanding his army and, after a battle outside Rome, revived the ancient office of dictator. He used it to proscribe (eliminate) thousands of opponents, rewriting the constitution to make it impossible for anyone to challenge the restored powers of the Senate. The guarantor of this regime was his own army, and when he retired in late 80BC, his reactionary settlement unravelled.

Above: Mithradates VI Eupator, King of Pontus (115–63BC), was one of Rome's most determined enemies in the east. His attempts to expand his Black Sea empire into Greece led to his defeat by Sulla and Lucullus, and he took his own life in 63BC.

THE END OF THE REPUBLIC
60–30BC

Julius Caesar was the third man in the secret but powerful triumvirate formed with Pompey and Crassus. Although a patrician, he supported the *popularis* faction, and was therefore hated by many in the Senate. However, he had made himself loved by the people through putting on lavish games, and had gained a reasonable military reputation in Spain. With the support of the other triumvirs he easily won election as consul in 59BC.

Once in office, Caesar quickly passed two land reform measures, giving Pompey's veterans their lands. He also revised taxes in the east, giving Crassus what he wanted for his own supporters, the tax-collecting knights. With Pompey and Crassus' support, his next step was to procure for himself proconsular command in the two important Gallic provinces (southern France and northern Italy) with their large armies, rather than the trivial command over "the woods and forests of Italy" that the Senate had decreed. Caesar pushed these measures through the Senate and Assembly ruthlessly and often illegally. It is reported that he once beat up his fellow consul Bibulus when the latter tried to oppose him. The support his fellow triumvirs had given him revealed the existence of their covert alliance, and Pompey married Julia, Caesar's daughter. Such political marriages were very common at the time.

THE END OF THE TRIUMVIRATE

In 58BC Caesar went north to take up his proconsular command and begin the lengthy conquest of Gaul, gaining for Rome one of its most important provinces. Meanwhile, the other two triumvirs were supposedly guarding his interests in Rome. The triumvirate was formally renewed in 56BC at Lucca. Crassus took up command in the east, keen for military glory to rival that of his fellow triumvirs. Disaster followed at Carrhae in 53BC. Crassus' legions were destroyed by the Parthians in the desert, and Crassus died with them. This left Pompey and Caesar in open and deepening rivalry, with the Senate backing Pompey as a lesser evil. In 49BC Caesar started civil war by crossing the Rubicon into Italy. Moving swiftly, he seized Rome, was appointed dictator by the people – in theory an emergency post – and followed Pompey and his other enemies to Greece, where he defeated them at Pharsalus in 48BC. Pompey, fleeing to Egypt, a nominally independent kingdom, was murdered upon arrival. Caesar, after encountering and being seduced by Cleopatra, then pursued and defeated the Republicans in Africa and Spain, celebrating a grand triumph in Rome while passing through.

Above: Julius Caesar, dictator

Below: Rich but defenceless, Egypt fell to Rome in 30BC.

CAESAR'S DICTATORSHIP

Once back in Rome, Julius Caesar embarked on a series of reforms including a general cancellation of debt and the founding of new colonies in Spain, Gaul, Greece and Africa – for his soldiers and the city's unemployed. He also reformed the calendar, began building the huge Basilica Julia, brought citizens from outside Italy into the Senate, started draining the Pontine marshes and reformed the currency – all this in a few months.

Early in 44BC Julius Caesar assumed perpetual dictatorship, revealing that his monopoly of power was not temporary, but permanent, like a king's. Like a king, too, was the way his image appeared on coins and statues. But this was anathema to all true Republicans. On the Ides (15th) of March 44BC, just before he left Rome for an eastern campaign, Julius Caesar was stabbed to death by a group led by Brutus, reputedly a descendant of the man who had driven out the last king in 509BC.

THE SECOND TRIUMVIRATE

Caesar's assassins, about 60 senators, had nothing realistic to put in his place, except more civil war. In the complex manoeuvrings that followed, Caesar's fellow consul, Mark Antony, formed the Second Triumvirate with young Octavian Caesar, the dictator's adopted son, and Lepidus, another Caesarean. Savagely proscribing many Republicans in Rome, they pursued the conspirators to Greece and defeated them at Philippi in 42BC. There followed a division of the empire, with Octavian ultimately taking control of all the west, and Antony controlling the east. Antony soon became enamoured of Cleopatra, the beautiful, intelligent queen of Egypt and the last Ptolemy ruler. Although officially married to Octavia, sister of his co-triumvir, Antony soon shunned her in favour of Cleopatra, and Octavia returned to Rome, humiliated.

Antony's military fame was tarnished by his failed campaign against the Parthians in 36BC. Meanwhile, Octavian was completing the basilica of the now deified Julius and establishing his own reputation as a patriotic Roman. The final showdown at the naval battle of Actium in north-west Greece in 31BC was an anti-climax, with many of Antony's supporters deserting. Pursued to Egypt, Antony and Cleopatra committed suicide, depriving Octavian of the joy of exhibiting them in his triumph, but not of the kingdom of Egypt, which he annexed personally. Two years later, Octavian returned to Rome to begin the immense task of the restoration of the Roman world after almost a century of civil war.

Above: The Battle of Actium in 31BC was the final stage in the long civil wars. Octavian's victory meant that the Roman world could at last be reunited and at peace after decades of civil wars. It also marked the completion of Rome's conquest of the Mediterranean world.

Below: The head of Julius Caesar on this silver denarius, a novel honour, shows the victor's laurel crown granted him by the Senate – which he wore all the time to disguise his growing baldness.

PEACE RESTORED: THE FIRST EMPERORS: 30BC–AD68

Above: Augustus, his family and friends are shown on the Ara Pacis, *or Altar of Peace, in Rome, in traditional Roman attitudes, symbolizing the restoration of "the Republic".*

Victorious after the long civil wars, Octavian finally returned to Rome in 29BC. His aim was to found a peaceful, effective but constitutional government, which the Republic in its last decades had failed to supply. The whole empire had suffered from the exactions of rival generals and was exhausted. As a cost-cutting exercise, he disbanded half his huge army, settling the soldiers in colonies around the empire. From now on, there would be a regular army of only 28–30 legions, or around 150,000 men, backed by equal numbers of auxiliary troops stationed in camps along the frontiers. To symbolize peace and to give the city room to grow, Octavian let most of the old Servian walls decay. Respecting Republican laws, he kept no troops in Italy – now extended to include the Po valley – but he retained nine cohorts of special Praetorian guards. Unlike Caesar, he seldom had a bodyguard in Rome. But he used his friends and colleagues, notably Agrippa, his general and son-in-law, and Maecenas, his cultural minister.

OCTAVIAN TO AUGUSTUS

In 27BC Octavian formally resigned his offices and announced "the transfer of the state to the Senate's and people's free disposal". He received them back with thanks, along with the title Augustus, meaning revered, auspicious, augmenting. He was elected consul and gave the Senate new powers as a high court and took part in its debates, becoming *princeps senatus*, leader of the Senate. Its functions became administrative, not political, in his disguised revolution. Augustus termed himself *princeps*, or first citizen, avoiding appearing royal or imperial. He gave up always being consul in 23BC after a serious illness. In its place, the Senate offered him tribunician power, making his person sacrosanct, and *maius imperium*, power over all the provinces. His *auctoritas*, personal prestige and authority, were key to his success, along with his old-fashioned probity, or *virtus*.

But the basis of Augustus' power was military, for he was also *imperator*, commander-in-chief. He used the army to expand the empire, annexing north-west Spain and the Danubian lands from the Alps to the Black Sea. Egypt also came under his control, while in the east he made a peaceful settlement with

THE HOUSE OF JULIUS AND CLAUDIUS

JULIUS CAESAR = Cornelia   Julia = M. Atius Balbus

Julia = Pompey the Great   Atia = C. Octavius

Marcus = Octavia = C. Claudius
Antonius   Marcellus

Scibonia = AUGUSTUS = Livia = Tiberius
                            Claudius Nero

M. Claudius
Marcellus

Marcus Agrippa = Julia = TIBERIUS   Drusus = Antonia the
                                           the elder   younger

Drusus the
younger

Gaius Lucius Agripps Julia Agrippina = Germanicus
               Postumus   the elder

Nero   Drusus   GAIUS   Gnaeus = Julia = CLAUDIUS = Valeria
Caesar Caesar (CALIGULA)   Domitius Agrippina   Messalina
                              Ahenobarbus

NERO = Octavia   Britannicus

the Parthians in 20BC. It was only in Germany that his expansionist policy was defeated when Varus was annihilated with three legions in AD9. This defeat plunged him into despair. His grandsons, his intended heirs, had both died and he had unwillingly adopted his stepson Tiberius of the proud Claudian family. None of the Julio-Claudian dynasty would ever repeat Augustus' golden age.

THE HEIRS OF AUGUSTUS

Tiberius, an excellent general, was an embittered man of 53 by the time he came to power in AD14. He continued Augustus' policies but lacked his *auctoritas* and charm. Instead, he relied on Sejanus, prefect of the Praetorian guard, as first minister, especially after Tiberius retired to Capri in AD26. There he was rumoured to indulge in fantastic sexual perversities. Probably untrue, such stories illustrate his unpopularity. Sejanus started treason trials that killed many in the imperial family before being executed for treason himself in AD31.

Tiberius' successor was his 24-year-old great-nephew Gaius, called Caligula after the little boots (a version of *caligae*, military boots) that he wore as a child. Very popular at first, Caligula abolished treason trials and proved as generous as Tiberius had been mean. But a serious illness six months into his reign seems to have driven him mad. He began a reign of terror, executing the Praetorian prefect Macro and many senators. His behaviour became increasingly eccentric – he joked he would make his horse consul. After he built a temple to himself as co-equal with Jupiter, he was assassinated in AD41.

While the Senate debated, a guard discovered a 50-year-old man hiding behind a curtain: this was Claudius, Caligula's uncle, passed over in the succession because of his bad stammer. But Claudius had a shrewd brain. Hailed by the Praetorians as emperor – he wisely offered them a bribe – his reign followed Augustan precedents, except for his conquest of Britain in AD43, which won

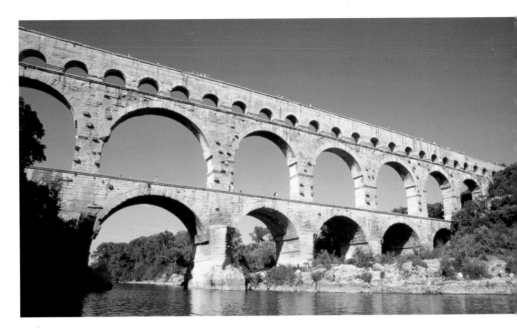

him military laurels. Claudius relied on freedmen as civil servants and began to centralize the government. But his personal life was less happy. His wife Messalina, notoriously promiscuous, was arraigned for treason in AD48. Claudius then married his niece, Agrippina, who probably poisoned him to make way for her son Nero.

Nero was only 17 when he succeeded his stepfather in AD54. At first guided by the philosopher Seneca and the Praetorian prefect Burrus, he ruled well, apart from murdering Britannicus, Claudius' son. He had artistic interests if not talents, and made a public performance as a singer in AD64. By then, with his mother murdered, Burrus dead and Seneca forced to commit suicide, Nero had become a tyrant to rival Caligula. The fire that destroyed half of Rome in AD64 was blamed on him by the people, although he scapegoated the Christians and had many of them burnt. He used the opportunity to build his Golden House, grandest of all the imperial palaces, but he also issued intelligent building regulations afterwards. Fatally, Nero neglected the army, and it was army rebellions that ended his rule in AD68. Abandoned even by his slaves, he committed suicide on 9 June AD68. The line of the Julio-Claudians died with him and civil war flared once again across the Roman world.

Above: The Pont du Gard, supplying Roman Nimes in southern France, is among the grandest surviving aqueducts and a monument to the blessings of the long Augustan peace. Beginning in 30BC, this period saw unprecedented prosperity spread around the empire, especially in the west.

Below: This fresco from the Golden House, the huge palace Nero built in the centre of Rome, illustrates the myth of the birth of Adonis – and also the high quality of Roman frescoes at the time.

THE FLAVIANS AND "THE FIVE GOOD EMPERORS": AD69–180

Above: Scenes from Trajan's Column in the Forum in Rome illustrate his victories in the Dacian wars and also provide us with detailed examples of Rome's army at its zenith.

Below: In AD124 the emperor Hadrian ordered the completion of the vast Temple of Olympian Zeus in Athens, started 650 years before. Hadrian favoured Athens in many ways, eventually becoming its archon *(mayor).*

Vespasian, emperor AD69–79, emerged victorious from the civil wars of AD68–9. A member of the Flavian family, his father was of equestrian not senatorial rank, but Vespasian proved a far better ruler than many Julio-Claudians. On reaching Rome in October AD70, he found that the state was almost bankrupt. To fill the coffers, he increased taxation and so earned a reputation for meanness – he even taxed the disposal of urine. Vespasian restored the frontiers and strengthened the eastern defences. He recruited from among non-Italians both for the Senate and the administration and made no pretence about the monarchical nature of his regime – only his sons could succeed him. He kept the consulate, still much coveted by senators, almost completely in the Flavian family.

Titus, who succeeded in AD79, had to deal with the Vesuvian eruption. Catastrophic and costly, it was fortunate for posterity, as it preserved Pompeii and Herculaneum almost intact. Charming and lavishly generous, Titus was generally popular and he completed the immense Flavian amphitheatre, or Colosseum, in AD80. But he died suddenly in AD81 and his younger brother Domitian, emperor AD81–96, succeeded him.

In some ways Domitian was an effective ruler, at least outside Rome. He extended the frontiers in south-west Germany and perhaps wisely curtailed Agricola's attempted conquest of Scotland. But at home he assumed a despotic manner, building a huge palace to rival Nero's. Becoming increasingly paranoid, he started a reign of terror that eventually led to his assassination in AD96.

THE ZENITH OF ROME

Domitian's successor, the elderly senator Nerva, realized that the army resented his accession and adopted Trajan, governor of upper Germany, as his son and heir. Trajan's reign (AD98–117) saw the empire at its peak geographically and perhaps economically. He was called *optimus princeps*, best of emperors, by the Senate. His building programme rivalled Augustus', while his care for the poor and sick showed a new imperial compassion. But Trajan was primarily a great soldier. Between AD101–6 he crushed the aggressive kingdom of the Dacians, finally annexing their land (Romania) and settling it with colonists. He then turned east, first annexing Arabia Petraea (Jordan), before dealing with Parthia, the old enemy in the east. Initial successes saw Roman armies reach the Gulf – their furthest advance. Mesopotamia (Iraq) and Armenia were added to the empire in AD115–17 but then abandoned.

Hadrian, Trajan's (probably) designated successor, spent much of his reign outside Rome, travelling round the empire. He visited Britain in AD122, building a

Left: Hadrian was the most peripatetic of emperors, traversing the empire from Egypt to Britain. Outside Rome at Tivoli, he also created the most spacious and luxurious of imperial palaces, with pools, colonnades and even temples – often replicas of what he had seen on his extensive travels.

Below: "Five Good Emperors" of the Adoptive and Antonine dynasties ruled Rome at its zenith in the 2nd century AD, adoption solving the problems of succession.

76-mile (122-km) long wall, to keep northern barbarian Britains out of the Romanized south. Hadrian admired Greek culture, and in Rome he built the Pantheon, one of the finest of all Roman temples. His successor, Antoninus Pius (emperor AD138–61), was an elderly senator who never left Italy. Under him the empire slept in a prosperous calm.

THE FIRST CRISIS

Ironically, under Marcus Aurelius, AD161–80, one of the last great pagan philosophers, Rome was engaged in a series of conflicts. The army was so weakened by the plague of AD166 that invading Germans were able to cross the Alps, while another band almost reached Athens. In a long series of wars, Marcus went on the counter-offensive, intending to annex what is now the Czech Republic and Slovakia. At the same time, he let some Germans settle inside the empire. He was still campaigning on the Danube when he died in AD180. He left the throne to his son Commodus: it was to prove a disastrous choice.

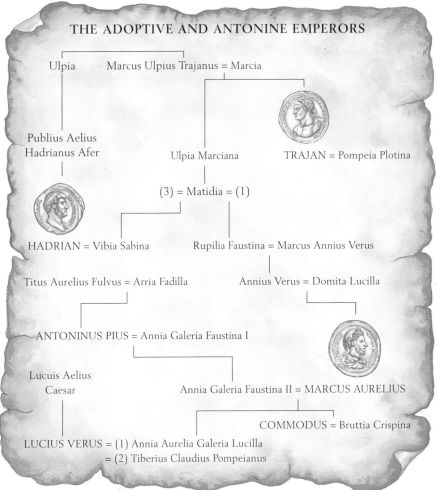

THE ADOPTIVE AND ANTONINE EMPERORS

Ulpia   Marcus Ulpius Trajanus = Marcia

Publius Aelius Hadrianus Afer

Ulpia Marciana   TRAJAN = Pompeia Plotina

(3) = Matidia = (1)

HADRIAN = Vibia Sabina   Rupilia Faustina = Marcus Annius Verus

Titus Aurelius Fulvus = Arria Fadilla   Annius Verus = Domita Lucilla

ANTONINUS PIUS = Annia Galeria Faustina I

Lucuis Aelius Caesar   Annia Galeria Faustina II = MARCUS AURELIUS

COMMODUS = Bruttia Crispina

LUCIUS VERUS = (1) Annia Aurelia Galeria Lucilla
= (2) Tiberius Claudius Pompeianus

CRISIS AND CATASTROPHE
AD180–284

Above: Under the debauched and incompetent Commodus, here shown dressed as the hero Hercules, the Golden Age ended in renewed civil wars.

Below: Septimius Severus, who came from Libya, founded a new dynasty that, through its Syrian connections, lasted for 40 years and produced a remarkable range of emperors.

Aged only 18, Commodus was the first emperor to inherit the throne from his father since Titus. Although Marcus Aurelius had groomed his son for his imperial role, Commodus soon shunned onerous public duties, ruling through all-powerful favourites. After an assassination attempt in AD182, he was reluctant to appear in public at all, preferring to spend his time in his palaces or country villas, where he indulged in sexual debauchery. When the last favourite, Cleander, had been sacrificed over a grain shortage in AD190, Commodus returned to Rome, where he ordered the deaths of many prominent citizens. His assassination in January AD193 caused fresh civil wars.

When Septimius Severus, commander of the Danubian legions, reached Rome in April AD193 two earlier claimants had been killed already. It took him four more years of wars before he defeated his rivals in the east and west and began reforging the monarchy. The first emperor of African origin (he came from Libya), Severus was essentially a soldier. He increased the army's size and improved its pay and conditions of service. He ruled as an autocrat, stationing a legion outside Rome and killing 29 senators. But as a general he was brilliant, leading an attack on Parthia in AD197, which captured the capital Ctesiphon (Baghdad). He died in AD211 in York after a northern campaign. On his deathbed, he reportedly told his two sons Caracalla and Geta to "pay the soldiers and ignore the rest".

Although Severus had told his sons to work together, Caracalla soon murdered Geta. Caracalla's reign, AD211–17, is notable for his law of AD212 which gave Roman citizenship to all free males in the empire. This law was probably passed for its taxation potential, as Roman citizens paid death duties, but nevertheless it was a significant move in the widening of Roman privileges. He also constructed the most grandiose baths in Rome.

Assassinated in AD217, Caracalla left no heirs, but the Syrian branch of the Severan family produced a 14-year-old boy, Elagabalus, whose reign (AD218–22) is notorious for his sexual promiscuity. This promiscuity was supposedly in honour of the Syrian sun god Baal, whose orgiastic worship Elagabalus introduced to Rome. His marriage to a Vestal Virgin impressed neither Senate nor people. Aware of the dangers, his grandmother Julia Maesa turned to another grandson, Alexander Severus, who became emperor at the age of 14 after Elagabalus' murder by the army.

Alexander reigned for 13 years – reigned rather than ruled, for real power lay with his mother, Julia Mammaea. She enlisted the Senate's support, but he failed to win the army's loyalty. An unconvincing general, he and his mother were murdered in AD235.

THE HOUSE OF SEVERUS

Publius Septimius Geta = Fulvia Pia

Julius Bassianus

(1) Paccia Marciana = SEPTIMIUS SEVERUS = (2) Julia Domna

Julia Maesa = Julis Avitus

Gaius Fulvius Plautianus

Julia Soaemias = Sextus Varius Marcellus

Julia Mammaea = Gessius Marcianus

CARACALLA = Plautilla

GETA

L. Seius Sallustius

ELAGABALUS = (1) Julia Cornelia Paula
= (2) Julia Aquila Severa
= (3) Annia Faustina

Sallustia Barbia Orbiana = ALEXANDER SEVERUS

THE 30 EMPERORS

In the 50 years of chaos that followed, at least 30 emperors, perhaps more, were proclaimed by armies around the empire. Assassination became the norm, as different armies – from the Danube, Syria and the Rhineland – fought each other, rather than the enemy. Barbarians responded with massive invasions, which worsened the economic and financial collapse. For a time, the whole concept of one empire looked doomed: the western provinces broke away to form the Gallic Empire from AD260 to 274, while the eastern provinces were overrun by a resurgent Persian empire under a new dynasty, the Sassanids. Rome's revival owed much to emperors from Illyria (the Balkans), who proved more energetically patriotic than the Romans themselves.

In AD248 the emperor Philip the Arab celebrated Rome's millennium, but there was little to celebrate. (Philip himself was murdered the following year.) The Goths, formidable horsemen from Sweden, crossed the Danube and ravaged the Balkans, Asia Minor and Greece. Plagues swept the empire, while the Persians, under Shapur I, invaded the eastern provinces and took Antioch, the great eastern trading metropolis.

Valerian, who became emperor in AD253, was captured in AD260 by the Persians, ending his life in humiliating captivity. However, his son and co-emperor, Gallienus, reorganized the army into a far more mobile and effective force. He annihilated a Gothic force in the Balkans in AD268, but was murdered shortly after. Gallienus' work was continued first by Claudius II, who again defeated the Goths before dying of the plague, and then by Aurelian, emperor AD270–5, who crushed two German invasions of Italy. Aware that Rome itself was threatened, Aurelian hastily erected the city walls that still bear his name. In AD272 he recaptured the eastern provinces seized by Zenobia, queen of the oasis trading city of Palmyra. Two years later he defeated the last of the separatist Gallic emperors, Tetricus, reuniting Gaul with the empire. However, in AD270 he had to abandon Dacia as it was too exposed to invasion.

Aurelian promoted the worship of the Unconquered Sun, a semi-monotheistic deity to which he built a huge temple in Rome. He tried to restore the economy by issuing a new coinage. Inflation had reached terrifying levels – 1,000 per cent in the 17 years before AD275 – and the currency was almost worthless. This had led to payment in kind by the passing armies exacted from the peasants through whose lands they marched, or from the equally oppressed cities they were meant to be defending. Figures are lacking, but the economy and population of the empire shrank sharply during the chaos. However Egypt and North Africa did relatively well because they suffered few barbarian incursions. Emperor Aurelian was assassinated in AD275 but, although the empire half-relapsed into civil war, enough of his work remained for Diocletian, a soldier from Illyria, to use it as a base for reorganizing the government when he became emperor in AD284.

Above: The emperor Septimius Severus, here shown with his family, was the first Roman ruler to come from Africa, a part of the empire he favoured with lavish building projects and by advancing the frontier far into the Sahara.

Below: This bas-relief from Bishapur, Iran, shows the Persian king Shapur I humiliating the Roman emperor Valerian, who had been ignominiously captured in AD260.

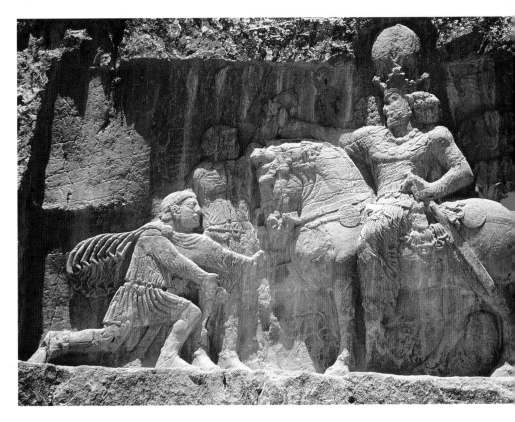

RECONSTRUCTION AND REVIVAL: AD285–363

Above: The tetrarchs, the four rulers of the Roman empire, are here shown embracing each other in unshakeable amity. This system worked only while its founder, Diocletian, remained the senior emperor. Afterwards, the empire reverted to civil wars.

With Diocletian (reigned 284–305AD) the ravaged Roman world entered a period of relative stability and even revival. But in the long term this was at the cost of personal liberty, as the emperors strove to create a quasi-totalitarian state to counter the chaos of the preceding age. Diocletian, a soldier, became emperor in a bloody coup. He thought the problem of defending different frontiers would be helped by having more than one emperor. In AD286, he invited a comrade, Maximian, to become joint emperor and rule the western half of the empire. Both men took the title Augustus. In AD293 he added two junior emperors, with the title Caesar: Constantius I to rule under Maximian in the west and Galerius in the east. The Caesars became the official heirs to the Augusti and each emperor established his own court: Constantius at Trier; Maximian at Milan; Galerius at Thessalonica and Diocletian at Nicomedia in Asia Minor. Rome, still the capital in theory, was ignored.

Each new capital was richly adorned with palaces and basilicas, and anyone approaching the emperor had to prostrate himself. This deification of the emperor was designed to overawe subjects and keep them in their place. The three sub-empires were not separate domains. They were all governed by the same laws and obeyed Diocletian, the senior Augustus. This system is called the Tetrarchy (from the Greek for four rulers) and at first it worked well.

LIFE UNDER THE TETRARCHY

In AD296, Galerius suffered a defeat on the troubled eastern frontier, but gained new lands the next year along the Upper Tigris. At the same time, Constantius invaded Britain, returning it to the empire after ten years of isolation. Such victories were helped by the tetrarchs' military reorganization. Each ruler had a mobile field force, the *comitatenses*, armoured cavalry who waged war. The other, larger, section of the army were the *limitanei*, permanent frontier troops who manned the much-strengthened border fortresses. German mercenaries became a regular part of the Roman army, and its manpower was increased to about 600,000 – twice its size under Augustus.

Such huge armies and courts cost money, and the tax burden became overwhelming. Diocletian tried to make reforms, issuing a new coinage in AD294,

Right: The dynasty of Constantine, who divided the empire between his three surviving sons from his marriage to Fausta, ruled the Roman world for nearly 30 years, although fratricidal strife rather than brotherly unity was the norm. Only Julian, Constantine's half brother, proved an able ruler.

THE HEIRS OF CONSTANTINE

Fausta (2) = CONSTANTINE I

CONSTANTINE II   CONSTANTIUS II   CONSTANS I   Constantina = Constantius Gallus

VALENTINIAN I

GRATIAN = Constantia

JULIAN THE APOSTATE = Helena

to re-establish people's faith in the currency ruined by constant inflation, but there were not enough new coins to have much impact. Then in AD301 he issued his Edict of Maximum Prices, to try to fix a maximum price for goods and services. This did not work either, for goods simply vanished from the shops and inflation continued. But he had more success in making taxes regular, with annual revisions, and introduced new assessment methods.

In AD303 Diocletian launched the last and greatest persecution of the Christians. Their numbers had increased steadily in the 3rd century AD, until about 8 per cent of the population was Christian. Diocletian, like many in the empire, felt that the Christians' rejection of Roman gods was treasonous to an emperor who styled himself "companion of Jupiter". First the Christian clergy, then the laity had to sacrifice to the gods or face imprisonment and even death. Tired of his rule, Diocletian then made the unusual decision to retire, abdicating in AD305 to grow cabbages in his palace at Split. He made Maximian retire too. Constantius then became Augustus in the west and Galerius in the east. According to the terms of the Tetrarchy, the idea was that the two Augusti would abdicate in turn, to be succeeded by their Caesars.

THE CONVERSION OF EUROPE

When Constantius I died in AD306, his son Constantine I was declared Augustus by the troops in Britain. In AD312 Constantine defeated Maxentius, son of Maximian, and 12 years later overthrew Licinius, Augustus of the east, thereby reuniting the whole empire. Reputedly, before defeating Maxentius, Constantine had had a vision of the cross. In AD313 in the Edict of Milan, he and Licinius granted religious freedom to all faiths, including Christians. By AD325 he was actively presiding over the crucial Council of Nicaea (Iznik), and by the time of his death in AD337 he had come to see himself as the thirteenth apostle.

In AD324 Constantine had established the city of New Rome, or Constantinople (Istanbul), as his new capital. The former Greek city of Byzantium, superbly sited on the river Bosphorus, became almost impregnable behind its double walls. Constantine continued Diocletian's policies, dividing the empire between his three sons at his death, when he was finally baptized a Christian. Of the sons, Constantius II emerged the victor of 15 years of civil war, but he was no general. Faced by barbarian invasions and usurpers, in AD355 he appointed his half-cousin Julian, known only as a scholar, as his Caesar in the west.

Julian proved almost a military genius, repelling German invasions in a series of brilliant campaigns. He also tried to lighten the burden of taxation on the wretched peasantry. Growing jealous of his success, Constantius tried to recall him, but Julian was declared Augustus by his troops in AD360. Civil war was averted by Constantius' death, and Julian, revealing himself a pagan, ordered the old temples be reopened. However, his reign was too short for this to have any effect, for he was killed on a Persian campaign in AD363. Both the house of Constantine and the pagan reaction died with him.

Above: These fragments of a colossal statue of the emperor Constantine illustrate how the later emperors liked to depict themselves: semi-divine absolute monarchs – very different from the modest image Augustus had displayed.

Below: The massive fortress-palace on the Adriatic at Split (Spalato), to which Diocletian retired to die in his bed, survives almost intact.

THE FALL OF THE WEST
AD364–476

Above: From the mid-3rd century AD onwards, Roman fortifications became vastly more massive and imposing. Behind the huge walls of fortresses such as this at Porchester on the English coast, Romans now passively awaited barbarian attacks.

Right: The imperial dynasty founded by Valentinian I saw a further acceptance of the division of the empire into east and west. Disaster occurred when his brother Valens, the eastern emperor, was killed at the battle of Adrianople. Theodosius I founded another imperial dynasty but one dependent on Gothic support.

After his death in AD363, Julian was succeeded briefly by Jovian, and then by Valentinian I, who for military reasons divided the empire, with his brother Valens taking the east. Both men were fine soldiers and Christians, but while Valentinian was religiously tolerant, his brother fiercely persecuted pagans and non-conformists. Valentinian proved the last really effective emperor in the west, repelling and avenging German invasions until he died in AD375, leaving his young and incompetent son Gratian as his heir. Meanwhile, far-distant events were leading towards catastrophe.

In AD378, in a defeat by the Goths at Adrianople (Idirne), Valens and most of the finest Roman troops were killed. Gratian then appointed a Spanish officer, Theodosius, as Augustus in the east, who let the Goths settle *en masse* with their own rulers within the empire. In theory, they supplied men for the Roman army but in practice they proved uncontrollable. Theodosius defeated rebel emperor Magnus Maximus in Gaul, reuniting the empire, but he was called "the Great" chiefly for his ardent Christianity. In AD392 he banned all forms of pagan worship, as intolerance became official .

Theodosius, last emperor of a united empire, died in AD395, leaving the empire to his incompetent sons: Arcadius in the east, who died in AD408, and Honorius, who lived to AD423, in the west. But the real ruler of the west was Stilicho, of German descent. In December AD406 the Rhine froze solid; Vandals and other Germans poured across it and spread into Gaul and Spain. The Rhine garrisons that should have repelled them had been withdrawn to face a usurper from Britain. The Rhine frontier was never restored and Britain, too, was soon abandoned. But there were more pressing problems in Italy. Stilicho was murdered by Honorius in AD408, and in AD410 Alaric, the Visigoth king, sacked the city of Rome.

Although the Visigoths were relatively restrained in their conquest – they were Christians, respecting churches and nuns – the world was profoundly shaken. For

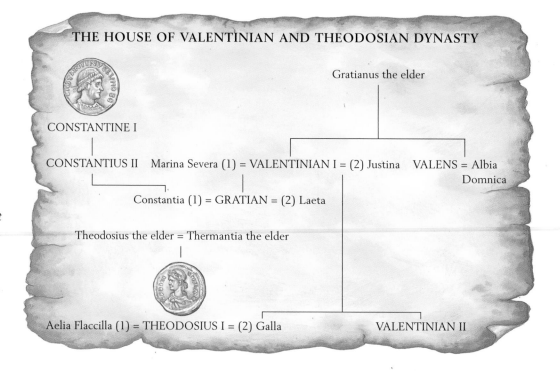

THE HOUSE OF VALENTINIAN AND THEODOSIAN DYNASTY

Gratianus the elder

CONSTANTINE I

CONSTANTIUS II   Marina Severa (1) = VALENTINIAN I = (2) Justina   VALENS = Albia Domnica

Constantia (1) = GRATIAN = (2) Laeta

Theodosius the elder = Thermantia the elder

Aelia Flaccilla (1) = THEODOSIUS I = (2) Galla   VALENTINIAN II the first time in 800 years, Rome had fallen to the barbarians. Alaric stayed only three days, leaving with much booty and Galla Placidia, the emperor's half-sister. Alaric died soon after, and the Visigoths moved into southern Gaul. Constantius, a general, then took command and forced the Goths to return Placidia. After suppressing other rebels in Gaul, he married Placidia, against her will, and was proclaimed co-emperor in AD421. Constantius III died late that year and his son, Valentinian III, became emperor in AD425. Under his mother Placidia's control, Valentinian reigned for 30 years, and the empire continued to disintegrate.

HUNS AND VANDALS

The best efforts of Aetius, another Roman general, could not prevent the Vandals establishing themselves in North Africa. Gaiseric, the Vandal king, captured Carthage, the second city of the western empire, in AD439 and built a pirate fleet to terrorize the whole Mediterranean region. But Aetius' attention had been drawn north by an even worse threat.

The Huns, frighteningly effective horsemen, had built an empire from the Volga to the Baltic. Their greatest king, Attila, known in history as "the scourge of God" (*flagellum dei*), ravaged the eastern empire's European provinces in

BYZANTIUM SURVIVES

If the Roman empire collapsed in the west, it flourished in the east. Thanks partly to Constantinople's superb defensive position, the east Roman or Byzantine empire (the name comes from the original Greek city) lived on for another thousand years. Although invasions had stripped it of its outlying provinces by the 7th century AD, it remained wealthy and civilized, wholly Greek in language and deeply Christian in its religion. A Russian ruler married one of the last Byzantine princesses, assuming the title Czar, or Caesar.

the AD440s and then turned west. Attila retreated after a day's bloody fighting at Châlons-sur-Marne in AD451. This was the one defeat of his life. The next year he headed towards a defenceless Rome. Pope Leo I met him unarmed and the two talked in Attila's tent. What they said is not known, but the Huns turned back across the Alps. Two years later, Attila died and his empire collapsed.

After Aetius' death in AD454, Rome was once more leaderless, and the Vandals viciously sacked Rome. Increasingly, it was German chieftains who made and unmade emperors. Finally, in AD476, Romulus Augustulus, the last emperor of the west, was deposed by the German Odoacer, who declared himself king of Italy. The empire had ended in the west.

Above: The Hunnish king Attila, "the scourge of God", became known as the most terrifying of the barbarian invaders of the 5th century AD, renowned for his savagery. He was not the most effective invader, however, for he did not sack Rome and his empire died with him.

ANNO DNI M·D·XXI AN
SARTIVS PINGEBAT
IT A·D·M·DLXXXII·ALO
ALEXIVS SEVERATV

CHAPTER II

GREAT ROMANS

The Romans of the early Republic were shadowy figures of whom not much is known. A typical example was Cincinnatus. He was working on his farm when called on to become dictator and save the city in 458BC. Wiping the sweat from his brow and putting on his toga, he went off to be emergency ruler and defeat the most threatening enemies. That done, he returned to his plough.

Such self-effacing patriotism could not survive Rome's rise to world power from the 3rd century BC. The influx of wealth and contacts with the sophisticated Greeks gave Romans, too, the desire and opportunity to excel as individuals, to shine on the stage of politics or the arts, to become famous generals, politicians, philosophers or poets. The poet Horace, writing in the 1st century BC, was as much concerned with his posthumous literary fame as Julius Caesar was with his prestige and power when he was alive. Almost inevitably, the only Romans we know much about today came from the political or intellectual elite. We have almost no written records of other Romans to flesh out what archaeology tells us of their lives. What writings have survived, however, are enough to reveal much about the inhabitants of the world's first global city. Soldiers and statesmen, writers and thinkers, and powerful women, all come alive in the pages of historians such as Tacitus and Suetonius, which are at times as racy and bizarre as today's gossip columns.

Left: Julius Caesar, the most famous Roman of them all, receiving tribute from ambassadors of client states.

GREAT ROMAN GENERALS

Above: Scipio Africanus, who defeated the Carthaginians first in Spain then in Africa, was typical of many great generals of the Republic in the jealousy and attacks his feats roused back in Rome. These finally forced him into premature retirement.

While military service was a customary, indeed often inescapable, part of life for most Romans in the Republic, a few commanders stand out, either for saving the state or for transforming the armies. Some went on to intervene in civilian life, usually with disastrous consequences.

PUBLIUS CORNELIUS SCIPIO AFRICANUS (235–183BC)

Scipio was only 25 years old when given command of the Roman armies in Spain. Facing an invincible Hannibal in Italy, the Republic had decided to attack Hannibal's base, but the first Roman army sent to Spain was defeated and both commanders killed. They were soon avenged. Scipio captured Cartagena, the Carthaginian headquarters, in 209BC. The next year, he defeated Hasdrubal, Hannibal's brother, by using light troops as a screen for the heavier legionaries. Soon all of Spain went over to Rome, while Hasdrubal was later defeated in Italy. Consul in 205BC, Scipio then led an army to Africa and defeated Hannibal at the Battle of Zama in 202BC, overcoming Hannibal's war elephants by ordering his legionaries to open ranks and let the maddened animals pass between them.

Scipio made two significant military reforms. First, his armies in Spain adopted the short Spanish stabbing sword. Devastatingly effective, it became the standard weapon of Roman legionaries. Second, he reformed the maniple, of which there were 30 to each legion, at times allowing them to act in three separate lines. More than a mere soldier, Scipio was among the first Romans to appreciate Greek culture and to learn the language properly. Partly because of this, he was subject to persecution by Roman traditionalists such as Cato the Censor. In 190BC, accused of misappropriating booty from the Syrian campaign, he finally withdrew from public life altogether.

GAIUS MARIUS (158–87BC)

A great soldier but a disastrous politician, Marius came from an equestrian family. He made his fortune as a *publicanus* (tax-collector), and he was a tribune of the plebs in 119BC, and praetor in 116BC. He was appointed commander of the armies in Africa in the wars against King Jugurtha. Brilliantly successful, Marius became consul in 107BC, finished the war in 105BC and was made consul again the next year.

Marius was given sweeping powers, which he used to reorganize the army, introducing the cohort of six centuries (500–600 men), and giving each legion its silver eagle, which soon became an emblem of tremendous importance. He made the *pilum*, the throwing spear, break at its neck, to render an enemy's shield useless. Marius abolished the last property qualifications so making the army more attractive to the poor, who now, however, had to carry all their equipment – hence their nickname "Marius' mules". These soldiers looked to their general, not the Senate, for reward. Marius used his remodelled army to crush barbarian invaders.

Returning to Rome, Marius got entangled in the struggles between the *populares*, whom he supported, and the conservative optimates, and fled from Rome when Sulla marched on it. He finally returned to Rome – totally illegally – at the head of an army in late 88BC. Becoming consul for the seventh time, he slaughtered his opponents before dying in 87BC.

Right: Marius reorganized the army, giving each legion its silver, later gilded, eagle, which became the focus of intense loyalty.

Although Marius had shown that military competence did not lead to a successful political career, his political success was nevertheless unprecedented at this time. Despite the rules of the constitution, he had been consul seven times, five of them consecutively.

LUCIUS CORNELIUS SULLA (138–79BC)

An optimate, or senatorial reactionary, Sulla came from an old but impoverished patrician family. Appointed general by the Senate for the war against Mithradates of Pontus in 88BC, he used his army to march on Rome and expel the *populares* – the first military intervention in Roman history. He marched on Rome again in 82BC with a devoted army of 100,000 men. The proscriptions that followed became notorious. Sulla executed 40 senators, 1,600 equestrians (knights) and many other citizens, giving their lands to his veterans. To enact his revolutionary programme, Sulla became perpetual dictator.

He passed measures that robbed tribunes of their power, removed courts from the knights' control and issued new treason laws. All this was done to boost the powers of the Senate, which he expanded to 600 men. Behaving in many ways like a monarch – Sulla inaugurated a huge building programme, repaving the forum and rebuilding the Temple of Capitoline Jupiter – he suddenly resigned all power in 80BC and retired, dying a year later. His settlement at once began to collapse, his career serving as both a warning and an example to later Romans.

MARCUS AGRIPPA (63–12BC)

Augustus' greatest general and later his son-in law, Agrippa came from a modest background but from 44BC he was Octavian's closest companion and his indispensable military adviser. He was responsible for building and commanding the fleet that defeated Sextus Pompeius at Naulochus in 36BC, and for defeating Antony's much larger fleet at Actium in 31BC. He did this by using Liburnian galleys, which were smaller and much more manoeuvrable than the giant quinqueremes in Antony's fleet.

In 33BC Agrippa accepted an aedileship – although he had already held the consulship, the top post. In effect, he became Rome's first water commissioner: he erected the first public baths, supervised the extension and rebuilding of the *cloaca maxima*, the ancient drain of Rome, and built an artificial reservoir, or *stagnum*. Later he built a network of roads across Gaul. After Marcellus' death, Agrippa married Julia, Augustus' only daughter, and their two sons Gaius and Lucius became Augustus' official heirs. Agrippa died on 20 March 12BC, one of the finest generals and ministers who had helped transform the Republic into the Principate.

Above: Sulla, the dictator

Below: The capture of Reggio, a Greek city in Italy, as depicted by a medieval artist.

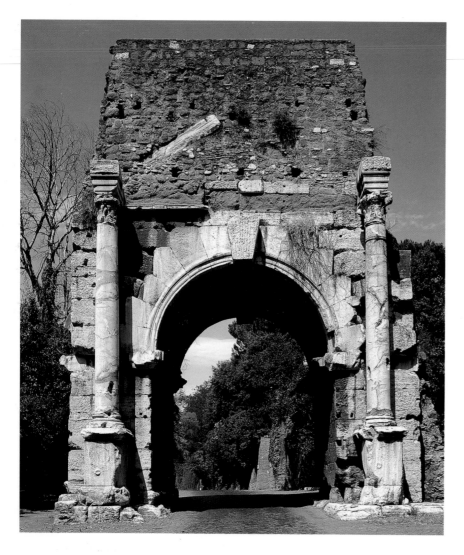

Above: A 3rd-century AD arch in Rome traditionally attributed to Drusus' victories.

Below: Germanicus

NERO DRUSUS (40–9BC)

The younger son of Livia and the stepson of Augustus, Drusus was the descendant of some of the proudest patricians in Rome and, like his older brother Tiberius, he was a formidable general. He first won military fame campaigning in Illyria. After the death of Agrippa in 12BC, although still in his early twenties, he was entrusted with the steadily advancing conquest of Germany. Drusus crossed the Rhine and invaded northern Germany, conquering territory up to the Elbe, which was designated as the new frontier. It is said he longed for the *spolia optima*, the highest military honours awarded to those who had killed an enemy commander in person, and so rode round the battlefields in search of a German chieftain to be his victim. This was probably slanderous, but he was certainly ambitious.

In 9BC Drusus' ambitions were curtailed by his early death in a riding accident. His death deprived the Julio-Claudian dynasty of a good general who was less morose and suspicious than his elder brother. It also deprived those senators still hoping for a republican restoration, for Drusus, according to Tacitus, was believed to be a secret republican. He had married Antonia, the daughter of Mark Antony and niece of Augustus, and they had two sons: Germanicus, who became a popular general, and the bookish Claudius, who later became emperor.

GERMANICUS (15BC–AD19)

The charming and popular son of Drusus and great-nephew of Augustus, Germanicus grew up partly among soldiers. Unlike his infirm brother Claudius, he was marked out early both as a general and as the successor to his father's reputed republican sympathies. By the time Tiberius became emperor in AD14, Germanicus had been appointed by Augustus as commander-in-chief of the Rhine forces, and Tiberius had had to adopt him as his son and heir.

At eight legions, the Rhine command was much the biggest in the army. Many of the legionaries had mutinied, and Germanicus restored order only with great difficulty and at peril to his own life. He led his armies into Germany, where Varus had lost his life and three legions in AD9. Germanicus buried some of the bones of the dead legionaries and defeated the German leader, Arminius, in a minor victory. However, Tiberius had no intention of resuming a forward policy, and in AD16 Germanicus was recalled. Tacitus has him say, "I achieved more by diplomacy than by war…as for the Cherusci and other savage tribes, Rome's vengeance has been asserted and we can leave them to quarrel among themselves." This proved true. In May AD17 Germanicus celebrated a triumph in Rome, then became consul with Tiberius before being sent to sort out problems in the east. On the way he visited Egypt, thereby arousing Tiberius' wrath, for senators were barred from Egypt without imperial permission. In Syria he soon quarrelled with the new governor, Gnaeus Piso.

When Germanicus died at Antioch in October AD19, it was rumoured that Piso had poisoned him. Whether scapegoat or villain, Piso was tried for murder and he committed suicide soon after. Germanicus left three children by his wife Agrippina, Augustus' granddaughter, of whom one survived to become emperor: Caligula, the vile antithesis of his charming, urbane father.

GAIUS JULIUS AGRICOLA
(AD40–93)

One of Rome's finest generals, Agricola was fortunate in having the historian Tacitus as a son-in-law to laud his life and career. Born in AD40 at Forum Iulii (Fréjus), Agricola's father was a senator and his mother a cultured woman who sent him to Greek schools in Marseilles. He first served as a military tribune in Britain under Suetonius Paulinus (AD58–61). As quaestor to Salvius Titianus, governor of Asia, he was shocked by the "mutual covering up of malpractice" among officials. After holding office in Rome, he returned to Britain as a commander. Governorship of Aquitania (south-west France) was followed by consulship under Vespasian.

When he became governor of Britain (AD77–83), Agricola, under orders from Rome, decided to complete the conquest of Britain. He first subdued North Wales before overawing the Brigantes in AD79 by sending two military columns on either side of the Pennines. He continued north into central Scotland, reaching the Tay. In AD82 he turned south-west, conquering that corner of Scotland and glimpsing Ireland, which he optimistically thought could be conquered by a single legion. In AD83 he continued north along the eastern edge of the Highlands, building forts as he went. Finally, in AD84 he met

the gathered Caledonian clans at Mons Graupius, perhaps near Inverness, defeating but not annihilating their forces. He then ordered the building of a major legionary fortress (for more than 5,000 men) at Inchtuthil above the Tay. But the emperor Domitian, suddenly needing troops for the Danube, recalled a legion and the conquest had to be abandoned. "Britain was completely conquered and immediately let go", was Tacitus' bitter comment, but the Highlands would have proved very difficult to conquer and hold.

Agricola was also a great peacetime administrator. He built over 1,300 miles (2,200km) of roads and 60 forts, repressed abuses, notably in the tax-collecting system, was lenient towards minor offences but hard on major ones, and encouraged the Romanization of Britain. According to Tacitus, he "encouraged individuals and communities to build temples, fora and houses… He had leading Britons' sons educated in the liberal arts… The result was that people who had rejected Latin now sought to be fluent and eloquent in it." Such eloquence was a vital Roman civic skill and spurred the development of a true Romano-British aristocracy. Agricola had no further important commands under the increasingly paranoid emperor Domitian, but at least he kept his life.

Above: The great popularity of the general Germanicus at the time of his sudden death in AD19 led to many arches being raised in his posthumous honour across the empire, such as this one at Pompeii in southern Italy.

Below: One of the greatest generals and governors of the Principate, Agricola conquered almost all Britain but suffered Domitian's jealousy. This Renaissance portrait, if more imaginative than accurate, testifies to his fame.

JULIUS CAESAR
101–44BC

Above: This silver denarius with the head of Caesar – then a novelty in Republican Rome – dates from 44BC, the year of his assassination.

Below: The Forum and, bottom right, the Basilica Julia, which became Rome's chief law court and was perhaps Caesar's most imposing monument, although it was actually completed after his death by his heir Augustus.

Julius Caesar is probably the most famous Roman of all. Due to his early death, he achieved little as a ruler compared with his successor Augustus, yet he deserves his fame, for he was one of Rome's greatest generals and most far-sighted politicians. As a man, he was charming, urbane and often unscrupulous. As a politician, he was the first emperor in all but name. His career demonstrated that only monarchy – whether king, dictator or emperor – could save Rome from chaos. The charisma of his name, Caesar, was such that all his successors called themselves by it, even when totally unrelated to him. This practice continued long after the empire had ended and well beyond its reaches: in Germany up to 1918 (Kaiser is German for emperor) and in Russia (Czar also means emperor).

Gaius Julius Caesar was born on 13 July 101BC. Although a patrician, he was not from the highest Roman nobility. His marriage to Cornelia, daughter of Lucius Cornelius Cinna, linked him with the Marian *popularis* party, making him a wanted man under Sulla's dictatorship, so he withdrew to Asia. Returning to Rome after Sulla's death, he began his political career relatively slowly, supporting the repeal of Sulla's measures. He became quaestor in 68BC and aedile in 65BC, when he gave unusually lavish public games, both alarming the Senate and becoming heavily indebted to Crassus, Rome's richest man. He was now the leading *popularis*. In 63BC he became *pontifex maximus*, the chief priest of Rome, a prestigious post without many priestly duties. After becoming praetor in 62BC, and propraetor (governor) in Spain, he became a consul in 59BC, despite fierce senatorial opposition.

CONQUEROR OF GAUL

Caesar's election as consul was partly due to the support of Crassus and Pompey. Together the three men formed the First Triumvirate, initially a secret pact, always unofficial and essentially illegal. But Caesar's acts helpful to Pompey and Crassus revealed the existence of the triumvirate, so Caesar married his daughter Julia to Pompey to cement the alliance. Caesar often behaved unconstitutionally, forcing his conservative colleague Bibulus to resign. Caesar then got himself extended proconsular command in the "two Gauls".

The Roman provinces of Transalpine and Cisalpine Gaul (southern France and northern Italy) provided good recruiting grounds and opportunities for glory in Gaul itself, a huge area inhabited by warring Celtic tribes. After a victory over the Helvetii in 58BC, Caesar went on to defeat tribe after tribe. Although some

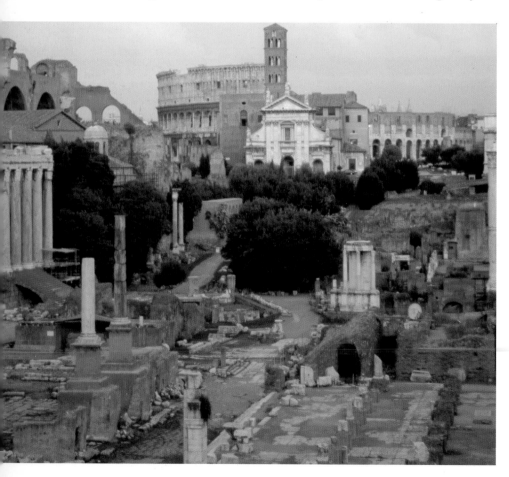

senators objected, the people loved his victories. No Roman had set foot in Germany before. Nor had they in Britain, Caesar's next target. His first invasion fleet in 55BC was damaged by tides, but he returned the next year with a larger force of five legions ferried by 800 ships. This force impressed the Britons, and Britain was claimed as a conquest. A huge final revolt in Gaul was suppressed in 52–1BC. The human cost was immense – over half of all Gauls of military age were killed – but Roman power had reached northern Europe. And Caesar had created an effective army, loyal only to him.

The triumvirate had been renewed in 56BC, but the deaths of Julia in 54BC and Crassus in 53BC undermined it. Pompey, jealous of Caesar, refused to let him stand for consul *in absentia* and gain immunity from prosecution. Caesar had either to accept political and even personal oblivion, or start civil war. On 10 January 49BC Caesar reluctantly marched his army across the Rubicon, the frontier of Italy. Civil war had restarted.

THE MAN AND THE DICTATOR

If slow to start war, Caesar was extremely fast to wage it. After an Asian blitzkrieg he uttered three infamous words "*Veni, vidi, vici*" (I came, I saw, I conquered). However, he spent the winter of 48–47BC besieged in Egypt, where he made Cleopatra his lover and installed her as queen.

As dictator in Rome he initiated a vast range of reforms. He overhauled the calendar, he cancelled interest on debts, and started construction of a basilica and forum. He ordered the draining of the Pontine Marshes and cutting of the Corinth Canal, but neither was accomplished. Around 80,000 landless Roman civilians and as many veterans were settled in 40 colonies around the empire. He issued a new coinage with his head on it and gave lavish games. The Senate was expanded to 900 with non-Italians from Gaul and Spain. A huge new library for Greek and Latin literature was planned. While he was preparing for a war with Parthia,

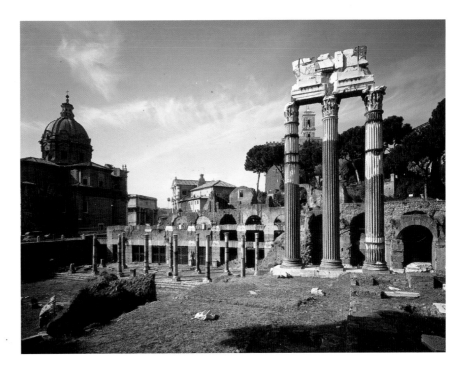

60 senators, led by Marcus Brutus and Cassius, stabbed him to death outside the Theatre of Pompey on 15 March 44BC.

Caesar had wrongly assumed everyone was won over by his generosity. One of the conspirators, Decimus Brutus, was named in his will and scheduled to be consul. But Caesar's growing personality cult was an outrage to republican sentiment; he had gone about with a large bodyguard, and when offered a regal diadem had not refused it convincingly. Caesar paid for his misjudgement with a life he may not have been too keen to prolong; he suffered from epilepsy and his health was worsening. Rome paid for it with another two rounds of civil war.

Caesar was tall, well built with dark eyes. Somewhat vain, he was delighted when the Senate voted that he could always wear a victor's laurel crown, as he was going bald. He was a noted womanizer but because of a youthful homosexual episode, he was throughout his life unable to escape being taunted with accusations of effeminacy. He was among Rome's best orators and a fine historian. A patron of the arts, he was perhaps the closest Rome produced to a "Renaissance man". His career has been an inspiration and a warning for many later rulers.

Above: Among Caesar's many projects for Rome was his new forum and a temple to Venus Genetrix, the goddess from whom the Julian dynasty claimed descent.

Below: This bronze statue at Aosta in northern Italy shows Caesar as the assured and triumphant general – a role he played to perfection.

POMPEY: CAESAR'S RIVAL
106–48 BC

Above: Pompey the Great. Undoubtedly a brilliant general and fine imperial administrator, in Roman politics Pompey often showed himself as being unable to decide between saving or overthrowing the Republic.

Below: Pompey was totally defeated by Caesar's numerically inferior armies at the Battle of Pharsalus. He fled to Egypt, only to be killed upon landing.

Caesar's greatest rival and one of Rome's finest generals, Pompey ended his career as the last defender of the Republic. Yet his own ambitions were fundamentally not so different from Caesar's. If he had won the civil war, he too could have ended up dictator, although he showed little of Caesar's statesmanlike vision.

Gnaius Pompeius Magnus, Pompey "the Great", was born in 106BC to a noble family on the Adriatic coast. He joined the reactionary general Sulla in 83BC and helped defeat the Marian faction in Rome, killing thousands of civilians. For this Sulla reluctantly granted Pompey a triumph, although he dubbed him *"adulescentulus carnifex"* (little teenage murderer). Given command against Spanish rebels in 77BC, Pompey defeated them, returning to Italy in time to deliver the final blow to Spartacus' slave uprising. Crassus then united with him to demand the consulship in 70BC. As consuls, the two men undid most of Sulla's reforms, restoring the tribunes' powers and reducing the Senate's control of the law courts, winning popular support if senatorial distrust.

When pirates began threatening Rome's corn supply in 67BC, Pompey was given command of 120,000 soldiers and 500 ships. He divided the Mediterranean into twelve zones and within three months had solved the problem. The *Lex Manilia* gave him similar powers over the east, where a war against Mithradates of Pontus had dragged on. Pompey, taking over Rome's armies in Asia, led them to a series of sensational victories: Mithradates committed suicide and Pompey united his kingdom of Pontus with the province of Bithynia. He then marched east as far as the Caucasus, deposing or installing kings, making them client states of Rome and founding 40 new cities. Turning south, he deposed the

last Seleucid king and annexed Syria. Continuing into Judaea, he entered Jerusalem and even the Temple, to Jewish dismay. But he confirmed the Macabee dynasty on the Judaean throne, again as client kings. His settlement of the east was so well judged that it effectively lasted 120 years and boosted Roman imperial revenues by 40 per cent. In 62BC he returned to Italy, laden with glory and booty, with his victorious army behind him.

His return was feared, for he had been expected to emulate Sulla and march on Rome. Instead, he disbanded his armies and entered Rome as a civilian, expecting a triumph of suitable splendour and, even more important, land for his veterans. The Senate prevaricated for a year on the former and refused the latter. This proved fatal. Rebuffed, Pompey formed the First Triumvirate with his rivals, Crassus and Julius Caesar, marrying Caesar's daughter Julia to cement the alliance. As consul, Caesar gave Pompey's men their land, but his conquests of Gaul made Pompey jealous. During Caesar's absence, Pompey was effectively master of Rome, becoming sole consul in 52BC.

All he did with his power was to build Rome's first stone theatre, dedicated in 55BC, and side increasingly with the Senate, now dominated by Cato the Younger, a reactionary. When civil war broke out in January 49BC, Pompey reluctantly accepted command from the Senate. He retreated to Greece in the face of Caesar's superior forces, but at Dyracchium (Durazzo) he surrounded and nearly captured Caesar's army. However, in August 48BC he was decisively defeated at Pharsalus and, fleeing to Egypt, was killed as he stepped ashore. Pompey, a proud soldier if often uncertain of his course in Roman politics, might have preferred this end to being ignominiously pardoned by Caesar.

MARK ANTONY
83–30BC

Mark Antony (Marcus Antonius) was Julius Caesar's trusted follower, Octavian's rival, then his ally and finally his enemy. Lord of half the empire and greatest living Roman general, he was hailed as a god in Greek cities and achieved fame as the lover of Cleopatra, queen of Egypt.

Born in 83BC, Mark Antony started his career as an officer in Egypt in the 60s BC. From 54–50BC, he served under Caesar, becoming one of his most trusted officers. On the fateful Ides of March of 44BC, Antony was consul with Caesar and after Caesar's assassination, effectively became Rome's ruler. He used his position and rhetorical skills to drive the assassins from Rome but was outmanoeuvred by Octavian. Antony was too good a general to beat, however, and they came to terms. The Second Triumvirate was formed by Antony, Octavian and Lepidus, a necessary but powerless third. After the triumvirate had beaten the conspirators, Antony took the eastern half of the empire and Octavian most of the west.

From the start, relations were strained. Antony had greater prestige and larger forces but Octavian had Italy and Caesar's name. Antony married Octavian's sister, Octavia, and the triumvirate was renewed in 37BC. But it was obvious that Antony was entangled with a far more alluring woman, Cleopatra VII, queen of Egypt.

Cleopatra, Greek by culture and descent, was an intelligent woman and a shrewd ruler. Her wealth as much as her person initially attracted Antony, and he ostentatiously accepted her aid, ignoring Octavia whom he sent back to Rome. Deeply offended by this snub, Octavian began planning war and in 32BC read out what he said was Antony's will. In a ceremony in Alexandria, Antony gave many sub-kingdoms to Cleopatra's children by Caesar and himself, although confirming Pompey's eastern settlement.

Worse still, when Antony went north in 31BC for the showdown with Octavian, he took not only his Roman army and navy, but also Cleopatra, confirming his image of being under her thumb. In the stand-off between the two armies, Antony's men began deserting and the sea battle was an anticlimax. Both Antony and Cleopatra fled to Egypt, where they committed suicide when Octavian arrived in 30BC. If unsuccessful as rulers, Antony and Cleopatra became immortal as great lovers, not a fate that the great Roman general would have relished. Mark Antony's life ended in tragic failure. If he had triumphed, then an empire less narrowly Roman might have evolved.

Above: This statue in Vienna shows Antony as a debauched drunkard. In fact, he was a highly competent general.

Below: The banquets of Antony and Cleopatra, where pearls were dissolved in wine, were noted for decadence and luxury.

THE HISTORIANS' VIEW

Above: This bust of Caesar is unusually unflattering – unlike his two lively histories.

The Romans recognized the power of history – that an imperial nation needs an inspiring, unifying myth, which history alone can provide. Among the fathers of Western history, Roman historians believed an individual's actions counted and that writing history had a moral purpose. As Tacitus, the greatest Roman historian, wrote, "Virtues should not be silently ignored, while the perpetrators of wrong actions… should be threatened with disgrace before posterity."

JULIUS CAESAR (101–44BC)

Caesar called his histories of the Gallic wars and civil wars *Commentaries* rather than full-scale histories. Although they had an obvious political purpose, the histories remain very readable. Written in the third person in a plain, concise style that only rarely becomes monotonous, they tell the gripping tale of Caesar's remarkable campaigns, with interesting geographical and cultural discussions about the Gauls, a people to whom he was not unsympathetic. He also related and praised his men's deeds as well as his own. The civil war commentary, which was not wholly written by Caesar, was more openly a defence of his actions in precipitating civil conflict.

SALLUST (86–34BC)

An active supporter of Caesar in his youth, Sallust took to writing history after being forced out of politics. He developed a terse, epigrammatic style inspired by Thucydides, the greatest Greek historian, but unfortunately most of his works, relating the history of the Republic down to 76BC, are lost.

Sallust was concerned with virtue and he repeatedly attacked the corruptions of his age, especially those of the luxury-loving aristocracy. Sallust himself had been a radical tribune of the plebs, although he later became a highly corrupt provincial governor.

LIVY (59BC–AD17)

At the age of 30, Livy began writing his life's work: a detailed history of Rome. Made up of 142 books, running from Aeneas' (legendary) arrival in Italy to the death of Drusus in 9BC, only 35 books survive intact, with fragments of others.

Essentially a conservative patriot, Livy retained a belief in Rome's grand destiny that won him both Augustus' approval and lasting popularity. He was the historian Rome had been waiting for. His style varied from the majestic to the vivid, while his imaginative sympathy for Rome's opponents makes him a humane writer. He, too, believed that history must instruct and elevate as much as inform.

Although not consciously dishonest, at times Livy attributed words and feelings to his characters that he had no way of knowing were true. Due to his own lack of military experience and partly, perhaps, to his imperfect Greek, he also made several military mistakes. For example, in describing the battle of Zama between Hannibal and Scipio in 202BC, he

Below: Sallust turned historian only after leaving politics. His terse style recalls that of the ancient Greeks he so admired.

Above: The emperor Augustus approved of Livy's history of Rome's rise.

misinterpreted the Greek historian Polybius' description of Hannibal's third line as Italians, when they were in fact Hannibal's crack veterans from his Italian campaigns, held in reserve. But apart from this, and a tendency to accept legends of Rome's beginnings uncritically, he combined epic grandeur of language and lively description with the conscientious research of a true historian.

TACITUS (AD55–C.116)

Often considered the greatest Roman historian, Tacitus is admired and emulated by many subsequent writers for his style as much as his content. He came from northern Italy, where his father had been a tax-collector. He rose swiftly under the Flavians, entering the Senate under Vespasian and becoming consul in AD97 under Nerva. He wrote most of his histories under Trajan, his major works being the *Germania*, the *Agricola*, about his father-in-law, the *Histories* dealing with the Flavians and the *Annals* of the Julio-Claudians from AD14–64. Much of the last survives and forms a crushing, if unfair, indictment, especially of Tiberius, who slowly emerges as the brutal monster he always secretly was. Other characters – Sejanus, Claudius, Messalina, Nero – are also scathingly depicted. The action alternates between the imperial court at Rome and military camps on the frontiers and is filled with scenes of heroism or of villainy – with no mention of the provinces, which, for the most part, were growing peacefully richer. Tacitus was only interested in the grand themes of a period he saw as "rich in catastrophe, terrifying in its battles, rotten with mutinies". He carefully assessed all available sources before writing, but he was very biased, seeing Tiberius merely as Domitian's forerunner. His *Agricola*, by contrast, is a near eulogy focusing on Agricola's governorship of Britain, and ignoring almost everything else. His *Germania* paints the Germans as noble savages, in contrast to corrupt Romans. Master of the devastating postscript and

ironic put down, his style is intense and subtle, making him one of the great masters of Latin prose. His own gloomy fatalism stemmed from a nostalgic Republicanism coupled with an awareness that the empire had come to stay.

SUETONIUS (C.AD69–C.140)

The raciest and perhaps least serious of the major Roman historians, Suetonius is invaluable to posterity as he had access to imperial records that have since been lost. From an equestrian family, he rose in the imperial service, briefly becoming one of the emperor Hadrian's secretaries before his dismissal in AD119, reputedly for a scandal involving the emperor's wife. He spent the rest of his life writing. His two surviving works are *The Lives of Famous Men* and *The Lives of the Twelve Caesars*, the latter covering the Caesars from Julius to Domitian. He focused on highly entertaining, if not always reliable, accounts of each emperor's personal eccentricities, especially their habits in the bedroom or dining room, after dealing with the political events of the reign. He tended to highlight the former; for example detailing Caligula's remarkable antics in Rome while almost ignoring Claudius' conquest of Britain.

Above: One of the high points of Tacitus' Annals *describes the return of Germanicus's ashes, carried ashore at Brindisi by his widow Agrippina. Tacitus implied Tiberius had had his nephew murdered – almost certainly unjustly. But he hated Tiberius and blackened his reputation.*

Below: Suetonius took a racily biographical approach to history in his Lives of the Twelve Caesars. *He knew about court life, having been Hadrian's secretary.*

ROMAN PHILOSOPHERS
THE GREAT THINKERS

Above: Man of the world as much as philosopher, Seneca tried to apply Stoicism's noble tenets to real life – a doomed attempt that finally contributed to his death.

Below: Epictetus, shown in this medieval illustration talking to the emperor Hadrian, was one of the last and greatest Stoics.

In no area was Rome more indebted to Greece than in philosophy. This was perhaps inevitable, as philosophy was for long considered only a "footnote to Plato", the greatest Greek thinker. From the 2nd century BC on, many educated Romans studied philosophy in Athens, while the major schools of Greek philosophy, Epicureanism, Platonism and Stoicism, found imaginative adherents in Rome. They wrote in Greek as often as in Latin.

LUCRETIUS (C.96–55BC)

One of Rome's greatest poets as well as philosophers, Lucretius turned the dry, austere philosophy of Epicurus (341–271BC) into a lyrical, impassioned plea for a life free of political ambition and superstitious fears of death in *De Rerum Natura* (On the Nature of Things). Epicureans believed in avoiding political engagements, instead cultivating friendship in private communities. Radically, they admitted slaves and women as members, giving rise to ill-founded gossip. Far from indulging in orgies, they actually lived in sober modesty. The gods, according to Epicurus, exist but are unconcerned with human affairs, and human beings have free will. Lucretius writes with an intensity and richness of language, especially in his opening passage, "Delight of men and gods, life-giving Venus", which contradicts his supposed cool detachment. Epicureanism, although attracting the poet Horace, defied Roman belief in public service too deeply to spread far. Lucretius was Rome's great Epicurean poet but contributed little new in philosophy himself.

SENECA (4BC–AD65)

Although not an original thinker, Seneca, who also wrote plays, popularized Stoicism so successfully that his writings are still read today. Founded by Zeno (335–263BC), Stoicism taught universal brotherhood in harmony with a divine, rationally ordered universe. Seneca tried to live, and certainly died, according to his beliefs. Tutor, and also minister for five years, to the emperor Nero, Seneca was implicated in a conspiracy against Nero and forced to commit suicide, which he did with dignity and stoical courage. The essence of his teachings can be found in his letters to friends: "I was glad to hear that you live on friendly terms with your slaves, for so an intelligent, well-educated person like yourself should… Remember: the man you call your slave is of the same species and breathes, lives and dies under the same sky as you. You can imagine him as a free man, he can imagine you a slave… My advice in short: Treat your inferiors as you wish to be treated by your superiors." (*Epistulae Morales*, Moral Letters)

EPICTETUS (C.AD55–135)

As a slave, Epictetus was made lame by his master's abuse. He endured this without complaint, seeing the body as a mere "casing". Freed on Nero's death, in AD89 he was expelled from Rome and settled in Greece. He spent the rest of his life teaching an austere, yet compassionate philosophy. He attacked those who offered quick, easy cures for the human condition, believing that only those with the spiritual strength to cope with their own animal nature and with others' distressed souls and possessing the "counsel of God", could become true philosophers. He urged his followers to trust in divine providence through every misfortune, as he had. His ideas deeply influenced Marcus Aurelius.

MARCUS AURELIUS (AD121–80)

Plato's dream of an empire ruled by a philosopher-king seemed about to come true when Marcus Aurelius became emperor in AD161. Tragically, however, his reign was spent mostly in battles. His *Meditations*, written in Greek while on campaign, are the private records of a troubled man, who used philosophy to help him "as a man, as a Roman and as an emperor". They are also the last Stoic writings, but tinged with Platonism. "Say to yourself every morning: 'Today I shall encounter the officious, the graceless, the arrogant, the treacherous, the envious, the selfish. All this has affected them because they do not recognize the difference between good and evil.'" Marcus Aurelius had an absolute trust in divine providence and saw the universe as one great natural order whose laws men must accept and seek to understand.

PLOTINUS (C.AD204–70)

After studying philosophy in Alexandria, Plotinus settled in Rome, where he became a protégé of Gallienus, emperor from AD253. His writings, collected in the *Enneads*, were the most radically mystical since Plato's and today he is considered the founder of Neoplatonism.

Plotinus compared the universe to a huge fountain of light. An endlessly flowing source, the First Principle, the *monos*, or the One, descends radiantly like the light of the sun through ever lower levels of being until it reaches the very lowest, that of matter, at which point the cosmic dance moves back up towards the One. All human beings are capable of, indeed long for, reunion with the One, which Plotinus called "the flight of the One to the One" and claimed to have achieved three times. This can be experienced through inward contemplation rather than religious rites. Unlike the Stoics, Plotinus ignored completely the external world falling into ruin around him. Neoplatonism later influenced medieval, Renaissance and even Romantic thinkers.

Above: Philosophy continued to interest Rome's richer youths, here shown in debate with a philosopher on a 4th-century AD marble carving.

Above: Plotinus

ROME'S ENEMIES

As Rome's empire grew, it faced formidable opponents, both civilized and barbarian, who at times inflicted crushing defeats on its armies. But, until the empire finally collapsed in the west in the 5th century AD, Roman discipline, resilience and adaptability always won through and overcame earlier reversals.

HANNIBAL BARCA (247–183BC)

The Romans had no greater enemy than Hannibal, the Carthaginian general who came closer than anyone else to conquering them. While the First Punic War had been fought overseas in Sicily and North Africa, the Second was mostly fought in Italy, devastating the peninsula. The Romans called it "Hannibal's war".

Hannibal was the son of Hamilcar Barca, a Carthaginian general who established an empire in Spain to compensate for the loss of Sicily after the First Punic War. It is said that he made his young son swear enmity to Rome on the altar of Moloch, the chief Punic god, in Carthage. In 221BC, Hannibal took over the Punic army and attacked Rome's ally, Saguntum. Wrong-footing the Romans, who were themselves planning a Spanish expedition, he then marched through southern Gaul and crossed the Alps in late 218BC, braving snowstorms that killed most of his elephants. Emerging into Cisalpine Gaul, he defeated the Romans at Trebbia in December and the next spring routed Flaminius' army at Lake Trasimene. His third, most devastating victory against much superior forces came at Cannae in 216BC. He won this by his tactical genius and professional army, which feigned a retreat in the centre before outflanking the Romans.

After Cannae, some large cities – Capua, Tarento, Syracuse – joined Hannibal, but the majority of Rome's Italian allies remained loyal and the Romans refused to despair. The Senate reappointed Fabius Maximus as dictator, and he waged a war of attrition. Hannibal had no siege engines to attack the walls of Rome, even though they were manned only by boys and old men, and Carthage would not send enough reinforcements. When his brother Hasdrubal finally reached Italy with an army in 207BC, he was defeated separately and his head thrown into Hannibal's camp.

Hannibal maintained his mercenary army's loyalty for another four years with great skill and in increasingly hostile country, before being recalled to Africa. At Zama in 202BC he encountered Scipio, conqueror of Spain, and was beaten in open battle. Hannibal guided Carthage through the dark days after defeat, but his proposed reforms aroused fierce opposition and he went into exile, first in Syria, then in Bithynia, where he finally committed suicide to avoid capture by Roman agents.

He was undoubtedly one of the very greatest generals of the ancient world, resourceful, tenacious and indomitable, with a smattering of Greek culture, like many nobles in Carthage.

Above: Monument at the site of the battle of Cannae, where Hannibal's troops defeated the Roman army in 216BC.

Below: Hannibal led a multi-racial army over the Alps, with Spanish, African and Celtic contingents, along with his elephants, only a few of which, however, survived the passage. Here he rides a small north African forest elephant, a breed now extinct.

CLEOPATRA, QUEEN OF EGYPT (69–30BC)

Cleopatra VII, last of the Ptolemies, was portrayed to Romans as an oriental *femme fatale* who had lured the great Roman general Mark Antony to his downfall. In fact Cleopatra was Greek in language, culture and background, and she relied more on her intelligence and charm to captivate Caesar and then Antony than on her physical beauty. She wanted to acquire and then keep the throne of Egypt, and used Egypt's wealth to buy the support of Roman armies.

Cleopatra won Caesar's support against her brother Ptolemy XIII, supposedly her co-monarch, when he landed at Alexandria in 47BC. Legend says that Cleopatra was delivered wrapped in a carpet to Caesar's headquarters and they began an affair. Later, she had a son, Caesarion, by him. This liaison so enraged Ptolemy's supporters that they besieged the lovers in the palace. Part of the great library was burnt in the ensuing fighting, which led to Caesar installing her as sole monarch and a client of Rome. Cleopatra followed Caesar to Rome in 45BC, but returned to Egypt after his death.

When Antony met her, he was tempted as much by her wealth as her beauty, but he became her lover, the pair indulging in a life of sensual pleasure in Egypt, much to the delighted horror of opinion in Rome. After Antony had publicly snubbed his wife, the sister of his rival Octavian, he donated some provinces to his and Cleopatra's three children. Octavian's propagandists used this as evidence that Antony wanted to hand over the empire to Cleopatra – clearly not the act of a true Roman.

This famous love affair did not seem to affect Antony's plans for Rome's eastern frontier, but his political judgement was clouded. Instead of leaving Cleopatra behind when he assembled his troops for the final showdown, Antony let her come with him, leading many of his men to desert. The doomed pair escaped from Actium for a last winter of love, but Octavian followed. Cleopatra cheated him of his final victory by committing suicide, traditionally from an asp's bite, before she could be captured. Although Cleopatra may have affronted Octavian's puritanical patriotism, she presented little military threat to Rome.

Above: Antony and Cleopatra, the famous lovers, as played by Richard Burton and Elizabeth Taylor. The Roman soldier's and Egyptian queen's political views may have coincided also, for Cleopatra was determined to defend Egyptian independence while Antony perhaps envisaged a loose Roman hegemony over the east, not annexation.

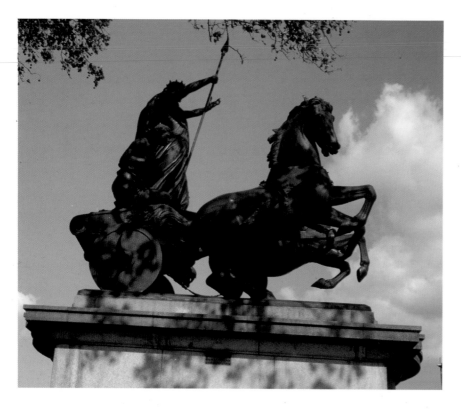

Above: Boudicca, queen of the Iceni, in her chariot. Her revolt against Roman extortions – which included the rape of her own daughters – threatened Rome's hold of Britain, but the Britons were too chaotic to overcome Roman discipline.

Below: This coin struck by Zenobia of Palmyra as empress of the east in 270AD does not do justice to the famed beauty of this descendant of Cleopatra. Like her ancestor, Zenobia was beaten by Rome in the end.

BOUDICCA, QUEEN OF THE ICENI (DIED AD61)

The Iceni, a warlike tribe of Britons, occupied what is now Norfolk. Their king, Prasutagus, had accepted Roman rule, effectively becoming a client king. On his death, Prasutagus left his kingdom equally to his daughters and to the Romans. The imperial procurator, Catus Decianus, however, expropriated all Iceni lands and allowed Roman *publicani* – taxfarmers – into the kingdom. According to Tacitus, when Prasutagus's widow Boudicca objected, she was flogged and her daughters were raped. Her outraged subjects then revolted and marched on Camulodunum (Colchester), traditionally led by their redoubtable queen. "In appearance she was very tall and most terrifying, with a fierce glance and harsh voice; a great mass of tawny hair fell to her hips", wrote Cassius Dio more than a century later. Camulodunum had no walls and the governor, Suetonius Paulinus, was far away in Anglesey with the main Roman forces. After sacking Camulodunum, the Iceni, along with other Britons, almost annihilated the depleted Ninth Legion sent against them and marched on London, already the trading centre of Britain. They burnt it, together with Verulamium (St Albans), reportedly killing 70,000 Romanized citizens. Then, somewhere in the Midlands, the now huge British force met the Romans under Paulinus with 10,000 men. The Britons were so confident of victory that they brought their wives and children along to enjoy the spectacle. But Roman discipline won the day; the drunken, half-naked Britons fell before the steadily stabbing Roman short swords, and the fugitives became entangled in their own wagons. The legionaries killed every child, woman and even ox they found. According to Tacitus, Boudicca committed suicide soon after. Her revolt had accomplished nothing, except encouraging the Romans to reform their administration in the island and get rid of the *publicani*.

ZENOBIA, QUEEN OF PALMYRA (REIGNED AD267–71)

In the prolonged crises of the mid-3rd century AD, Rome's eastern provinces were invaded by the Persians, who overran Syria, Mesopotamia and Asia Minor, taking the emperor Valerian captive in AD260. The Persians were repulsed not by Valerian's son, the emperor Gallienus, but by Odenathus, king of the wealthy oasis trading city of Palmyra, officially part of Roman Syria. Odenathus, controlling heavy cavalry and mounted archers, now became the semi-independent "Governor of the East". When he died in AD267, perhaps murdered, his widow, Zenobia, a gifted and beautiful woman who loved hunting and drinking, succeeded him. But she was not content with junior status. She annexed Egypt and much of Asia Minor, and in AD270 declared herself Augusta and her son, Vaballathus, Augustus. For a moment it seemed that Rome's whole eastern empire was lost. But the emperor Aurelian marched east and routed the Palmyrene armies, first outside Antioch and then near Palmyra, capturing Zenobia as she was fleeing towards Persia.

Traditionally, she was taken back to Rome, where she walked in golden chains in Aurelian's triumph, before being allowed to retire to a villa at Tivoli. Palmryra itself never recovered its old glory.

ATTILA THE HUN (C. AD406–453)

The *flagellum dei*, or "scourge of God", Attila has gone down in history as a ferociously bloodthirsty savage. The Huns, exceptionally skilled horsemen, had exploded across the Eurasian steppes in the 4th century AD. Their empire then stretched from the Urals to the Danube. Attila started by extorting money from the Eastern empire. In AD448 he reacted to a cut in this subsidy by ravaging the Balkans, defeating armies sent against him. In AD450, aware that he could not capture Constantinople, secure behind its new walls, he turned west with 70,000 horsemen, herding the terrified Germans before him. He crossed the Rhine in AD451 and ransacked Gaul. The Roman general Aetius hastened north and, with the help of the Visigoths, fulfilling their duties as federates, met the Huns at Châlons-sur-Marne. The battle, which cost the Visigothic king Theodoric his life, lasted all day, but at the end the Huns withdrew. It was the only defeat in Attila's life. Attila returned to winter quarters on the Pannonian plains. Here, in a city of tents, he lived in an odd mixture of squalor and luxury. His captives brought a veneer of Graeco-Roman civilization along with plunder of the empire. Attila himself, reputedly even dirtier than most of his people but with diplomatic abilities, enjoyed receiving Roman dignitaries, although the pleasure was probably one-sided. Next year Attila turned south and crossed the Alps, sacking Milan and Aquileia, whose fleeing inhabitants founded Venice as a refuge. Aetius had no troops to repel him now. Instead, Pope Leo I rode north and met the Huns. What the Pope said to Attila is unknown but possibly he reminded him of the fate of the last man to sack Rome. Attila turned back and died a year later from a burst blood vessel after celebrating his marriage to his latest wife, a young Frankish princess. Within a few years the Hunnish empire vanished and the Huns passed into history and legend.

Left: The great temple of Baal in Palmyra displays the sophistication and wealth of the city that challenged Rome in the east.

Below: Attila, advancing on Rome in AD452, reached and besieged Perugia in central Italy. No Roman forces could be found to oppose him, but Pope Leo I rode out to meet him and persuaded the Hunnish king to turn back, so saving Rome for that year.

CICERO
THE PEACEFUL ROMAN

Rome's greatest orator, lawyer and political thinker, Cicero was exceptional among the generals, consuls and warlords of the late Republic in never having been a soldier. He was, however, a fluent writer on subjects from astronomy to philosophy. Although his suppression of Catiline's conspiracy led to many citizens' arguably illegal deaths, he was a civilian and man of peace in an age of civil wars and naked military ambition. As his 800 surviving letters reveal, he was a man of genuine goodwill and optimism – over-optimism, as it turned out. Cicero attempted to apply Greek philosophy's ethical findings to Roman politics and human behaviour in general. Through Cicero's writings, much of Greek culture was transmitted to western Europe.

Marcus Tullius Cicero was born in 106BC in the small town of Arpinum, 60 miles (100km) south of Rome to a family of knights. None of his ancestors had held office in Rome, so his rise to the consulship made him a

Right: Cicero, a novus homo, *or self-made man, remains one of the greatest of all Roman writers and politicians, despite most unusually having no military career.*

novus homo, a "new"or self-made man. He depended on his skills as a lawyer and orator but luckily won the friendship and support of Atticus, a rich banker. Cicero started his legal career by appearing in court against one of Sulla's freedmen in 81BC, risking the dictator's wrath. Wisely, he withdrew to Athens to continue his study of philosophy. He accepted the ethical precepts of Stoicism that all human beings had a spark of the divine in them.

Returning to Rome after Sulla's death, Cicero was elected a quaestor in 75BC. The Sicilians, finding him honest, asked him to prosecute Verres, an ex-governor of the island, for extortion in 70BC. Cicero's speeches were so devastatingly effective, driving Verres into exile, that the grateful Sicilians showered presents on him. He distributed these to needy citizens. Cicero became a praetor in 66BC, dealing with legal cases "fairly and honestly", as Plutarch put it. He also advised Pompey, then assuming his high command. Finally, in 63BC he was elected consul, the highest office.

Cicero owed his meteoric rise, unsupported by any great noble house, chiefly to his mastery of rhetoric – dramatic, impassioned public speaking, a key art of ancient civilization. Brilliant at ridiculing opponents, he used wit, irony and innuendo to overwhelm and seduce listeners. He also embodied the aspirations of the rising commercial equestrian class. Realizing that the senatorial class was too narrow, Cicero envisaged a *concordia ordinum,* a concord of the classes between senate and knights, which he later widened to a *consensus omnium bonorum,* a consensus of all good men. He regarded himself as a saviour of the Republic by his swift if brutal suppression of the conspiracy by the disgruntled patrician Catiline, who tried to overthrow the state in October 63BC.

Unfortunately, Cicero failed to win over the one man with the military power to support his *concordia*. Pompey returned in triumph from his eastern conquests to be snubbed by the Senate. On meeting him, Cicero talked only of his own achievements, annoying Pompey. In 58BC Cicero was forced into retirement, accused of acting illegally over the Catiline affair. Although recalled by Pompey, his political influence never fully recovered and he had to write the co-triumvir Caesar a grovelling letter promising he would not attack him again.

THE WRITER

Cicero's enforced leisure gave him time to write. His letters, mostly to Atticus his banker friend, reveal an urbane and cultured upper-class Roman, fond of dinner parties and literary discussions. His letter describing the visit of Caesar to his villa near Puteoli is a masterpiece. "What a guest! Two thousand troops in all… The villa was sealed off. But it went off all right. He was in a good mood and all the talk at table was of literature. Political subjects were avoided altogether. But once is definitely enough".

Cicero was also a family man. His son Marcus was clearly a problem, getting through a vast allowance in Athens. Cicero reserved his greatest love for his daughter Tullia, whose death in childbirth desolated him. He tried to console himself with a belief in the immortality of the soul, but was not totally convinced.

Cicero wrote copiously on philosophy and politics – not original stuff, "only the exact words are mine". *The Laws, The Offices* and *The Republic* deal with politics and the constitution, while *De Finibus* (The Highest Ends) summarizes much of Greek philosophy.

After Caesar's death in 44BC, in which he had no part, Cicero persuaded the Senate to appoint young Octavian to lead an army against Mark Antony. This was a mistake. Octavian, forming the Second Triumvirate, added Cicero's name to the list of those to be proscribed (killed), realizing that Cicero represented the Republic's last best hope. Cicero had set out on a journey to join the conspirators in Greece when Octavian's men overtook him and cut his throat. His severed head and hands were later exhibited in the Forum.

Below: Cicero's humane and liberal views had a profound influence on later western writers, as this illuminated medieval manuscript attests.

CHAPTER III

THE
EMPERORS

Monarchs in all but name, the emperors of Rome
are among history's most remarkable, often most
colourful rulers, their unofficial position in control
of a supposed republic giving them intoxicatingly
unlimited powers. Originally reserved solely for
the Julio-Claudians, one of the great families
of the Roman nobility, the imperial throne gradually became the prize of other men. First there
were the Flavians, from small Italian towns, then
men born outside Italy, notably the Antonines, in
the 2nd century AD. Finally, in the 3rd century AD,
almost any halfway successful soldier might hope
– or fear – to be chosen as emperor by his armies.

Sometimes Roman emperors were model rulers:
among these imperial paragons Augustus, first and
longest-lived, ranks high, as do Trajan, Hadrian
and Marcus Aurelius. Balancing them are paranoids
and near-maniacs, such as Caligula; playboy-
buffoons, such as Nero; and the debauched –
Commodus and the almost indescribable
Elagabalus. Most emperors fall, like most human
beings, into a category neither good nor bad. So
Claudius, Vespasian and Domitian (initially but
not later), Septimius, Diocletian and Valentinian I
all proved humanly fallible. Undoubtedly, they
worked hard if increasingly ineffectually at their
task of governing the empire as they saw fit.
In the end, the task grew almost unbearably
onerous, becoming more a burden than a prize.

*Left: A general of the 3rd century AD commanding
his troops. The emperors remained above all army
commanders, military prestige being vital.*

EMPERORS OF ROME

Julio-Claudian emperors
Augustus 27BC–AD14
Tiberius AD14–37
Gaius (Caligula) AD37–41
Claudius AD41–54
Nero AD54–68

Year of the four emperors
Galba AD68–9
Otho AD69
Vitellius AD69

Flavian emperors
Vespasian AD69–79
Titus AD79–81
Domitian AD81–96

Adoptive and Antonine emperors
Nerva AD96–8
Trajan AD98–117
Hadrian AD117–38
Antoninus Pius AD138–61
Marcus Aurelius AD161–80
  and Lucius Verus AD161–9
Commodus AD180–92

Above: Vespasian

Above: Titus

Above: Domitian

Above: Trajan

Above: Hadrian

*Above: Marcus
Aurelius*

Above: Augustus

Above: Gaius Caligula

Above: Claudius

Above: Nero

Above: Tiberius

Civil war
Pertinax AD193
Didius Julianus AD193

Severan emperors
Septimius Severus AD193–211
Caracalla AD211–17 and Geta AD211
Macrinus AD217–18
Elagabalus AD218–22
Alexander Severus AD222–35

Emperors of the age of chaos
Maximinus Thrax AD235–8
Gordian I AD238
Gordian II AD238
Pupienus and Balbinus AD238
Gordian III AD238–44
Philip the Arab AD244–9
Decius AD249–51

Trebonianus Gallus AD251–3
Aemilius Aemilianus AD253
Valerian AD253–60
Gallienus AD253–68
Claudius II "Gothicus" AD268–70
Quintillus AD270
Aurelian AD270–5
Tacitus AD275–6
Probus AD276–82
Carus AD282–3
Numerian AD283–4
Carinus AD283–5

"Gallic" emperors
Postumus AD260–9
Laelianus AD269
Marius AD269
Victorinus AD268–71
Tetricus AD271–4

The tetrarchs and their successors
Diocletian AD284–305
Maximian AD286–305 and AD307–8
Constantius I AD305–6
Galerius AD305–11
Severus II AD306–7
Maxentius AD306–12
Maximinus Daia AD310–13
Licinius AD308–24

Above: Septimius Severus

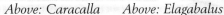

Above: Caracalla   *Above: Elagabalus*

Emperors of the house of Constantine
Constantine I AD306–37
Constantine II AD337–40
Constans AD337–50
Constantius II AD337–61
Julian AD361–3

Jovian AD363–4

Valentinian I (east) AD364–75
 and Valens (west) AD364–75
Gratian AD367–83
Valentinian II AD375–92
Magnus Maximus (usurper) AD383–8
Eugenius (usurper) AD392–4

Theodosian emperors
Theodosius I AD379–95
Arcadius (east) AD395–408
Honorius (west) AD395–423
Constantius III AD421
Theodosius II (east) AD408–50
Valentinian III (west) AD425–55

Last Western emperors
Marjorian AD457–61
Anthemius AD467–72
Romulus Augustulus AD475–6
Julius Nepos AD473–80

Eastern emperors
Marcian AD450–57
Leo I AD457–74
Zeno AD474–91
Anastasius AD491–518
Justin I AD518–27
Justinian AD527–65
Justin II AD565–78
Maurice AD582–602
Heraclius I AD610–41

With the advent of Heraclius, it becomes customary to talk of Byzantine rather than east Roman emperors, as the empire itself finally ceased to be Latin-speaking, even in the army.

Above: Diocletian

Above: Constantine I

Above: Julian

Above: Theodosius I

Above: Justinian I

AUGUSTUS: THE FIRST ROMAN EMPEROR

The transition from ruthless battle leader to revered "father of his country" was one of the greatest achievements of Octavian, who became Augustus, first and greatest Roman emperor. In 44BC, the 18-year-old heir and adopted son of Julius Caesar, just assassinated, had only the lustre of Caesar's name as backing. Cicero, the leading senator, gave him an army command against Mark Antony. But Octavian soon changed sides to form the Second Triumvirate with Antony, gaining mastery of the western part of the empire and, after defeating Antony at Actium in 31BC, rulership of the whole Roman world, just as Julius Caesar had.

In January 27BC, Octavian resigned all his powers, to receive them back, as pre-arranged, from a grateful Senate along with the title *Augustus* (literally revered). We call him the first Roman emperor, but to his contemporaries he took pains to seem no more than *princeps*, first citizen of the Republic. He disguised his power so carefully that his claim to have "restored the Republic" seemed almost credible. Typical of his apparent modesty was his home: an average-sized house formerly belonging to the orator Hortensius. It was located on the Palatine Hill, the traditional aristocratic area. His 45-year reign laid the foundations of a regime that lasted almost 250 years. This – revolution, disguised as a conservative restoration – was typically Roman.

Octavian was very unlike his great-uncle Caesar. Aware that Republican feeling was strong and wanting senatorial support, Octavian cultivated an image of traditional Roman *virtus*, which roughly translates as courage, virtue and probity. He needed the senators' and equestrians' help to run the empire – he had no proper civil service, merely a few secretaries. The 27BC settlement gave him proconsular power in provinces with large armies, such as Gaul (France) and Syria, run by legates appointed by him. Senators governed peaceful, unarmed provinces like Greece. The administration was thus depoliticized, but Augustus retained control of the army, and the title *imperator*, effectively commander-in-chief, from which comes the word emperor. His own military reputation was mixed: he relied heavily on capable generals such as Agrippa, but he retained the crucial loyalty of the armies. They swore loyalty to him, not the Senate, and remained remarkably loyal to his successors.

At first Augustus was consul almost every year, until illness in 23BC made him rethink his position. From then on he had "perpetual tribunician power", which allowed him to convene the Assembly and Senate and propose or veto laws. In 19BC he gained *imperium maius* (supreme power) giving him overall control in the provinces. His settlement was so effective that he faced only one feeble conspiracy. In 2BC he was declared *pater patriae*, father of his country, by the Senate.

Above: Although he had won power by the sword, Augustus stressed the civilian aspects of his regime by wearing a toga.

Below: A temple to Augustus was built after his death in Istria – he was not worshipped in Italy while he lived.

THE AGE OF AUGUSTUS

Contemporary writers saw the Augustan era as a golden age in almost every sense – politically, economically and also culturally. Augustus fostered the empire's economic recovery by restoring and ensuring peace. Guided by his cultural minister, Maecenas, he took a direct interest in cultural affairs, and Virgil's epic account of Rome's origins, the *Aeneid*, was a fruit of the age. A great building programme was inaugurated in Rome, completing Caesar's projects such as the vast Basilica Julia. In *Res Gestae*, his list of accomplishments, Augustus claimed to have restored or built 82 temples in one year, including one to Mars, the war god, and one to Apollo, the Greek god of poetry and science. Agrippa, his general, started Rome's first large public baths. Augustus boasted that he had found Rome a city of brick but left it a city of marble.

At heart, Augustus was a social conservative. He wanted to restore the traditional Roman virtues of piety and fidelity, or so propagandists proclaimed. He also wanted to raise the falling Roman birth rate. In the *Lex Julia* of 18BC, he made adultery a crime, penalized celibacy and childless marriages and gave tax breaks to families with three or more children. He banished even his own daughter, Julia, for adultery and the poet Ovid for general licentiousness. He also revived the sacred "secular" games and other old religious festivals.

THE MAN BEHIND THE IMAGE

Augustus was slim, rather short, but well proportioned, "unusually handsome and exceedingly graceful", according to Suetonius, with curly golden hair. Although his health was poor, he nevertheless lived to the age of 77. Ruthless in his youth, he later mellowed. He was a modest gambler and a sociable family man, enjoying dinner with friends. Surviving letters to Gaius, his grandson, calling him "my dearest little donkey", reveal paternal affection. His last years were unhappy, however. Not only did family problems distress him, but the Varus disaster in Germany in AD9, in which three legions were destroyed, shook him badly. He advised Tiberius, whom he had adopted reluctantly in AD4, to expand the empire no further. After his death in AD14 – almost certainly from natural causes – he was given a splendid funeral and declared a god by the Senate. He became the paradigm against which all later emperors would be measured.

FAMILY PROBLEMS

As emperor, Augustus inevitably involved his family in dynastic politics. In 36BC he married Livia Drusilla, who ignored his frequent infidelities and acted as a moderating influence on him. He had only one child, Julia, by his first marriage. Keen to pass on power to a direct descendant, he married Julia to his nephew Marcellus. When Marcellus died in 23BC, Julia, still only 16, was made to marry Agrippa, 24 years her senior. Their five children included two sons, Gaius and Lucius, whom Augustus adopted as his sons. But when Agrippa died in 12BC, Augustus turned to Tiberius, his gloomy stepson who was forced to divorce his wife, Vipsania, whom he loved, and marry Julia, whom he loathed, to be a guardian to the young princes. Disgusted, Tiberius withdrew from public life and Julia began a series of affairs which led to her exile. The premature deaths of the two young princes – Lucius in AD2, Gaius in AD4 – forced Augustus to recall Tiberius to favour. The resulting Julio-Claudian dynasty lasted until AD68.

Left: This cameo gemstone shows Augustus and the goddess Roma. Augustus was often worshipped in association with the goddess of Rome in the provinces but never in the city of Rome itself. After his death he was officially deified by the Senate.

Below: Augustus as the triumphant Roman imperator, *or commander-in-chief. In fact, he was not a brilliant general and in later years never led his armies in person, relying on his very capable generals.*

ORGANIZERS OF EMPIRE

Although the lives and reigns of some emperors were relatively undramatic, they played such vital roles in organizing or restoring the empire, expanding or stabilizing its frontiers and widening its citizenship, that they stand out as truly exceptional emperors. Two of the most notable were Claudius and Hadrian.

Left: On the assassination of Caligula, gangly, stammering Claudius was declared emperor by the Praetorian guard.

attempted and of which both Augustus and Caligula had talked. This proved remarkably successful. Part of southern Britain was overrun in AD43, and Claudius hastened north to celebrate its conquest. Conquests of Mauretania (north Algeria/Morocco) and Thrace in the Balkans made him the most expansionist emperor since Augustus and popular with the army and the people.

Below: The emperor Claudius is shown here in the guise of the god Jupiter – an implausible role for such a physically unimpressive and ungainly man, but one that became increasingly expected of all the emperors.

CLAUDIUS (REIGNED AD41–54)

Already 50 when the Praetorian guard declared him emperor on 24 January AD41, Claudius's appointment was an event that probably surprised him as much as everyone else. Tall, gangly, with a stammer and a tendency to dribble, Claudius had been kept in the background until his nephew, the new emperor Caligula, half-jokingly made him consul in AD37. After the assassination of Caligula, however, Claudius was the only Julio-Claudian available as next emperor.

Claudius was intelligent if bookish – he had written histories of the Carthaginians and Etruscans, which are now lost – and initially at least he had good intentions. He abolished treason trials and set about restoring public order, which had been shaken by Caligula's excesses, trying to work with rather than against the Senate. However, he had no military experience – a big disadvantage for a ruler whose power ultimately depended on the army, although his brother, the general Germanicus, was fondly remembered by soldiers. One of his first acts was to order the invasion of Britain, which Julius Caesar had

To please the volatile populace further, Claudius built an entirely new harbour near Ostia, with breakwaters and a lighthouse, greatly facilitating Rome's troubled grain supply. He also completed two aqueducts that had been started by Caligula. What displeased many in the Senate was his liberal policy of making "Gauls" – Roman citizens from Gaul, sometimes of Gallic ancestry but always Romanized – senators, and extending Roman citizenship widely. (Claudius himself was born in Lyons.) The Senate also criticized his reliance on Greek-speaking freedmen: Pallas looked after finance, Narcissus foreign affairs and Callistus the law. At first, Claudius kept his secretaries under control as they built up departments that foreshadowed the bureaucracy of the 2nd century AD. His love life was unhappy, however. His third wife, Messalina, on whom he doted, was 30 years younger than him and notoriously adulterous. She finally plotted to make one of her lovers emperor and was executed for treason in AD48. In his later years, in declining health, Claudius was ruled by his last wife, Agrippina, who probably poisoned him. Hostile historians have depicted him as hopelessly in thrall to his wives and freedmen, but provincials and later emperors like Vespasian remembered him as an unusually effective ruler.

HADRIAN (REIGNED AD117–38)

Perhaps Rome's greatest emperor devoted to peace rather than war, Hadrian is best known for his wall across northern England, but this is only one aspect of a many-faceted man. A distant relative of the emperor Trajan, whose niece Sabina he married, Hadrian was born in Spain in AD76. He distinguished himself in Trajan's Dacian campaigns and was governor of the key province of Syria during Trajan's eastern wars (AD114–17). When Trajan died, he was proclaimed, on rather debatable grounds, as his chosen heir.

Widespread Jewish revolts and Parthian counter-attacks led Hadrian to abandon all conquests east of the Euphrates, although he retained Dacia (Romania) and Arabia Nabatea (Jordan). He adopted a general defensive policy, personally overseeing the strengthening of the frontier defences in his journeys around the empire – he spent over half his reign outside Italy. On his British visit in AD122, he ordered the building of a stone wall 76 miles (122km) long and 20ft (6m) high, manned by 15,000 troops to keep the barbarians out of Romanized Britain. He also constructed less durable fortifications in Germany and Syria.

He built lavishly, reconstructing the Pantheon, Rome's finest temple, building his huge mausoleum (now the Castel Sant'Angelo) and a luxurious villa complex at Tivoli that included 160 acres (64ha) of gardens and pavilions. In Athens he added a new quarter to the old city, being such a passionate philhellene (lover of Greece) that he was nicknamed Greekling. Initiated into the Eleusinian mysteries, the most important in Greece, Hadrian became archon (mayor) of Athens, which he made head of a new Panhellenic League. He also ordered the completion of the immense temple of the Olympian Zeus, started by Pisistratus more than six centuries earlier.

Sexually Hadrian "ran to excess in the gratification of his desires", according to the 4th-century AD *Augustan Histories*, most notoriously in his passion for the beautiful young boy Antinous, who drowned mysteriously in the Nile. Hadrian thereupon founded a city in his lover's memory, Antinouopolis.

Hadrian got on badly with the Senate from the start, executing four senior senators early in his reign for alleged treason, and he was too obviously cultured to please the Roman populace. But he was a superb administrator and legal reformer. His jurist, Salvius Julianus, drew up a "Perpetual Edict", which codified previously unwritten laws. Hadrian also extended Nerva's and Trajan's policy of poor relief. Despite these achievements, he remained unpopular with the Senate, although there were no conspiracies against him while he was away on his long travels. The empire probably reached its economic peak during his reign, in which the eastern provinces finally recovered their political self-confidence and economic strength.

Above: Hadrian was one of the wisest and most conscientious, as well as cultured, emperors.

Below: Hadrian's most lasting achievement in northern Europe was the wall he built across northern England.

BEST OF EMPERORS

Above: Trajan was the most popular of all emperors.

Below: Trajan's Column in Rome celebrates and records his Dacian victories.

Traditionally, the reigns of the "Five Good Emperors" from Nerva to Marcus Aurelius (AD96–180) encompassed Rome's golden age. The differing fortunes of Trajan and Marcus Aurelius, the two great emperors at each end of the epoch, however, indicate that the empire was indeed passing through its zenith.

TRAJAN (AD98–117)

Born in Spain in AD53, Marcus Ulpianus Traianus was the first non-Italian emperor, although his family were Romans of senatorial rank. He was adopted as the son and heir of the emperor Nerva in AD97 as the elderly senator was so unpopular with the army. Trajan already had a distinguished military and civil record and proved an inspired choice. Affable and handsome, he was equally at ease with the Senate, people and army, but it was military matters that occupied him first.

In AD101 Trajan attacked Dacia (Romania), forcing Decebalus, the king of Dacia, to accept a humiliating peace. But Trajan renewed the war, and by AD106 he had captured the Dacian capital. Decebalus committed suicide. Huge quantities of Dacian gold were taken to Rome, along with Decebalus' head on a pole. Dacia became a Roman province, its lands settled by Romans, its gold mines protected by forts. In AD106 Trajan annexed Arabia Nabatea (Jordan).

With an improved and bigger army, Trajan turned to Parthia. Twin armies swept down the Tigris and Euphrates in AD115 to take the capital Ctesiphon (Baghdad). Trajan marched on to the Gulf, the only emperor to do so. Back home, the Senate voted him perpetual triumphs – a unique but empty honour. But he failed to take Hatra, a key city, revolts flared behind him and the Parthians counter-attacked. In AD117, his conquests across the Euphrates already abandoned, Trajan died of a stroke in Asia Minor.

THE GREAT BUILDER

Trajan was also a great peacetime ruler. He created special funds for helping poor children and built on a massive scale. Some projects were utilitarian, such as the new harbour at Ostia, and some were ornamental, such as his column, whose frieze relates his Dacian wars. Others, including his huge forum, his two libraries and his baths, were both. His correspondence with Pliny the Younger, governor of Bithynia, reveals Trajan's humane good sense. Although reputedly fond of boys and wine (as well as hunting and war), Trajan was never seen as drunk or promiscuous and there were few who disputed his right to the title *optimus princeps*, best of emperors, granted him by the Senate.

MARCUS AURELIUS (AD161–80)

Brought up by Stoic philosophers, high-minded, ascetic and self-sacrificing, Marcus Aurelius seemed destined to become Rome's true philosopher–king. But tragically his reign was filled with almost continuous warfare, and he spent much of it fighting. Born in Spain in AD121 to an aristocratic Roman family, Marcus was chosen as Hadrian's sole heir when he was only six. Antoninus Pius, the next (elderly) emperor, adopted him in AD138. Marcus became consul at the age of 18 and then Caesar (junior emperor). Lucius Verus, nine years younger, was his adoptive brother. When he became emperor in AD161, Marcus persuaded the Senate to make Verus co-Augustus alongside him.

Almost immediately, Parthia invaded Armenia. Lucius Verus went east and the Parthians were repelled – mostly by the governor of Syria, Avidius Cassius, Verus preferring the fleshpots of Antioch – and Ctesiphon and Seleucia-on-the-Tigris were sacked in AD165. The total destruction of the latter, a Hellenistic city, was thought to have aroused divine wrath, manifest in a terrible plague that the

Above: Marcus Aurelius, a philosopher by inclination, spent his reign in endless warfare.

Meanwhile, the Germans had rallied and Marcus had to continue his gruelling Danubian campaigns, spending each winter in camp, finding time between campaigns to administer the empire and write his famous *Meditations*. He decided to annex the whole area up to the Carpathians, forming a continuous new frontier that might prove more defensible. But his health, never strong, was now failing – he probably had cancer – and he died in camp near Vienna in March AD180. Commodus, his worthless heir, quickly abandoned his father's campaign and high ideals.

Below: The world-weariness of the philosopher–emperor Marcus Aurelius can be glimpsed even in these panels celebrating his (incomplete) triumph against the Marcomanni. The contrast with the unalloyed martial vigour of Trajan's celebratory column is very obvious.

victorious troops brought back with them. This ravaged the empire, weakened the army and overshadowed Verus' triumph.

An unexpected German invasion across the Danube, which reached Aquileia in north-east Italy in AD168, triggered a financial and military crisis. Marcus armed gladiators and slaves and went north with Verus. Lucius Verus' sudden death in AD169 did not affect operations, in which Marcus showed himself a very competent general despite having no earlier military experience.

THE DANUBIAN WARS

For five years, Marcus struggled with the Marcomanni and Quadi, Germanic tribes in the modern Czech Republic and Slovakia. He had almost defeated them, campaigning through bitter winters – one battle was fought on the frozen Danube itself – when a revolt by Avidius Cassius in Syria distracted him. Avidius had been misled by a rumour of Marcus' death into making a bid for the empire, in which the empress Faustina was perhaps involved. Avidius was murdered by troops loyal to Marcus before civil war could develop, so Marcus merely toured the east with his 14-year-old son Commodus before returning to Rome for a belated triumph in AD176. The column later erected by Commodus to mark this victory echoes Trajan's, but its overall atmosphere is sombre, rather than jubilant. Marcus rides his chariot with a weary, resigned air.

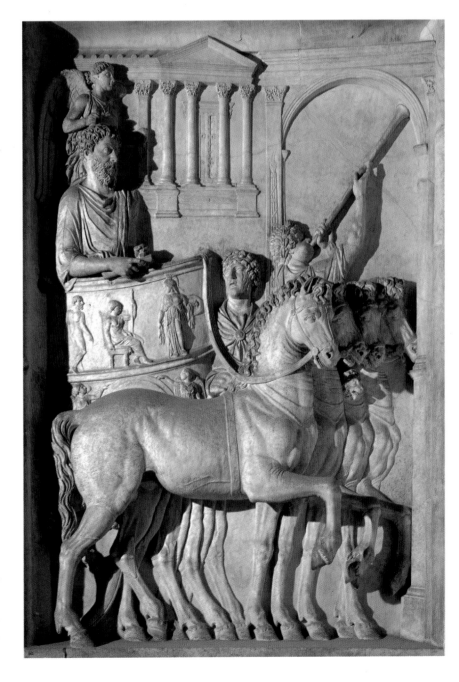

EVIL EMPERORS

The fact that the emperor's powers could appear unlimited encouraged some emperors – usually those who had inherited the throne young – to become power-mad or paranoid, or both, and to behave in ways that were capricious or despotic, if not arguably insane. Others, later in the empire, were simply brutal thugs, despite having undoubted military talent. All met violent ends.

CALIGULA (AD37–41)

When Augustus' great-grandson Gaius Caligula (literally "little military boots", a nickname he got from the boots he wore as a child) succeeded Tiberius in March AD37, Rome was jubilant. Aged 24 and son of the much-loved general Germanicus, Caligula promised to end the terror of Tiberius' later years. His reign started auspiciously: he recalled all exiles, burnt the police files and even made his uncle Claudius, embarrassingly clumsy, fellow consul.

That autumn, however, he became seriously ill, and when he recovered, his behaviour had changed completely. The illness could have unbalanced his mind, as Suetonius believed; alternatively, it could have brought out a latent paranoia and brutality. What appeared first was a reckless extravagance. He gave extremely spectacular games, at times appearing as a gladiator himself, and lavished attention on his favourite racehorse, Incitatus, who lived luxuriously in a marble stall. Caligula declared that he would make Incitatus a senator, even consul – only half a joke, for his relations with the Senate were deteriorating and in AD39 he dismissed both consuls for treachery. That summer he built a useless bridge of boats 2 miles (3km) long across the Bay of Naples and drove a chariot across it – a gesture typical of his extravagance, and perhaps indicative of growing insanity.

Spindly and prematurely bald, Caligula was insanely jealous of men with a good head of hair. Dressing in effeminate, gaudy silks, he generally did not impress people physically. Although he had had a military childhood, he felt his lack of military glory. In September AD39 he visited the Rhine legions before turning back abruptly, seemingly panic-stricken at being on the German side. He also talked of invading Britain, but when his army reached the Channel, he ordered the legionaries to collect seashells. After celebrating this "victory" over Neptune the sea god, he returned to Rome determined to be worshipped as a god himself. He built a temple to himself and forced senators to become its priests. Some historians suggest that in this he was emulating eastern monarchs, who were worshipped in their own lifetimes. Some emperors indeed were, but not in Rome. Finally, disgusted by such caprices, Caligula's courtiers and officers conspired to kill him on 24 January AD41 as he was leaving the games.

Above: Nero, the would-be artist and actual playboy, became one of Rome's most notoriously debauched and despotic emperors.

Below: The antics of Caligula introduced a capricious madness to the Principate that very nearly destroyed it.

NERO (AD54–68)

Just 17 years old when he succeeded the elderly Claudius in AD54, Nero promised to revive the spirit of Augustus' Principate. At first, guided by the philosopher Seneca, his former tutor, and the Praetorian prefect, Burrus, he seemed to rule well. Trajan later referred approvingly to Nero's first fine *quinquennium* (five years), although he may have been thinking only of Nero's building projects. Despite two family murders – the first in AD54 of his step-brother, Britannicus, the second of his mother, Agrippina, in AD59 – the new regime appeared to run smoothly enough.

In fact, Nero spent much of his time engaged with dramatic pursuits. For these he had a real passion if not talent, vastly admiring Greek culture, at least in its more histrionic aspects. At first Nero performed only before select private audiences, as a noble Roman forfeited all dignity by performing in public. He later alienated the upper classes by appearing on stage, first in half-Greek Naples in AD64, where he made his debut as a singer, and later in Rome itself.

After the death of Burrus in AD62, Seneca retired from court, aware that his influence over Nero was fading. Nero was free to give full vent to his passions, including satisfying his bisexual appetites and penchant for the rough trade. He had a boy, Sporus, castrated and then married him in a mock wedding ceremony. He abused married women and freeborn boys equally (slaves being thought "fair game"). Falling for Poppaea, wife of his crony (and later briefly emperor) Otho, he divorced and executed Octavia, Claudius' daughter, but then viciously kicked Poppaea to death in a rage. This last action lost him much popular support.

Nero's discovery of the senatorial Piso conspiracy against him in AD65 led to savage reprisals. When fire ravaged Rome in AD64, Nero was reputed – wrongly – to have started it and then "fiddled" or sung over the flames. In fact, his fireproof rebuilding regulations were very sensible but his new palace, the Domus Aureus (Golden House) appeared intolerably lavish and vast, sprawling over central Rome. To divert his unpopularity, Nero ordered the first recorded persecution of Christians. Most Romans had no fondness for this new sect but they grew disgusted when they saw Christians being coated with pitch and ignited as human torches in the circus to please the emperor.

Nero loved the glamorous absolutism of Hellenistic monarchies, but Rome was not ready for this. To pursue his artistic vocation, he went to Greece in AD66 and participated in the Olympic Games. He fell out of his chariot, but was declared the winner of every prize, the logic being that if he had not fallen out, he would certainly have won! By the time he returned, reluctantly, to Rome in late AD67, he faced revolts. Some collapsed of their own accord, but Nero dithered fatally, finally being declared a public enemy by the Senate. He committed suicide on 8 June AD68, crying, "What an artist dies in me!" Despite a few good ideas, such as cutting the Corinth Canal and restoring "liberty" (self-government) to the Greek cities, he had no concern or understanding of the army and left a half-bankrupt empire in the grip of civil war.

Above: Nero was popularly – but wrongly – supposed to have fiddled while Rome burned during the fire of Rome in AD64.

Below: After the great fire of Rome in AD64, Nero tried to make the newly recognized sect of the Christians into scapegoats. His plan backfired when their sufferings in the arena roused Roman pity.

Above: Domitian, the grim, sometimes paranoid, emperor

Below: Commodus posed as his favourite hero Hercules in the last years of his reign.

DOMITIAN (REIGNED AD81–96)

Depending on the observer, Domitian was an emperor whose reputation varied greatly. To the Senate and its supporters, including Tacitus, and also to many equestrians, he was an increasingly paranoid autocrat and priggish despot. To the army and to many people in the provinces, he was a conscientious and efficient emperor, albeit lacking the charm of his brother Titus, who had died after a reign of only two years. Although 30 years old when he succeeded Titus, Domitian had had little experience of office. He soon showed that he was a conscientious judge, if one of a marked puritanism. He forbade the castration of boys (for sexual purposes), and he punished homosexuality among senators. He also condemned to death four of the six supposedly chaste Vestal Virgins for having lovers, some incestuously. (One was buried alive in the traditional manner.) This was perfectly legal – as *pontifex maximus*, such cases were his responsibility – but the emperor's conservative rigour shook many in easy-going imperial Rome. What hurt the Senate far more was the way he openly treated them as mere subjects and demanded to be addressed as *dominus*, or lord. He assumed the title of Perpetual Censor in AD85 and summoned all his officials to the palace, rather than meeting them in the *Curia* (Senate House) or Forum. He rebuilt the imperial palace on the Palatine Hill in a style reminiscent of a Hellenistic monarchy – and Nero – where he entertained lavishly. Although he enforced a public puritanism, he kept many concubines himself, whom he personally depilated.

Aware of the need to keep his soldiers' loyalty, Domitian increased their pay by a third, and, lacking a military record, embarked on a perhaps unnecessary war in AD83 against the Chatti, taking the honorary title Germanicus for a modest victory. According to Tacitus (a biased source), only Domitian's jealousy prevented Agricola from completing his conquest of northern Britain in AD84. In fact, Domitian needed Agricola's troops to quell an uprising in the Danube region. Coupled with a senatorial conspiracy in AD87, this revolt made Domitian increasingly paranoid.

In AD93, fuelled by informers' reports that reached him in his palace – whose mirror-like walls allowed him to watch everybody – he began a reign of terror that spared none. Finally, his closest attendants turned against him, encouraged even by the empress, Domitia. He was murdered in the imperial palace on 18 September AD96. However, the army and Praetorians mourned him.

COMMODUS (REIGNED AD180–92)

Whatever the truth of the rumours that Marcus Aurelius was not the real father of Commodus and that the empress Faustina had slept with a gladiator, Commodus was certainly very unlike his industrious, disciplined and ascetic predecessor. Yet Marcus raised Commodus, his sole surviving son, as a future emperor, making him joint ruler in AD177.

Upon his accession in March AD180, Commodus abandoned Marcus' forward policy in central Europe. Back in Rome he soon showed his distaste for the tedium of government by handing over power to a series of favourites, usually his lovers. He later often had them executed to defuse outbursts of popular unrest. He meanwhile amused himself with his immense seraglio – allegedly containing 300 girls and 300 boys – mostly in luxurious villas outside Rome.

A botched assassination attempt in AD182, probably instigated by his elder sister Lucilla, fuelled his paranoia about the Senate, and he became more openly tyrannical. His chief favourite after AD185 was Cleander, a former slave from Phrygia (Asia Minor) who openly sold offices; in one year he sold the consulate 25 times, enriching himself with the proceeds. A severe shortage of grain in AD190 led to his downfall, when Commodus sacrificed him to the angry mob. In his last years, Commodus emerged from his seclusion to participate in gladiatorial contests – something that deeply shocked many Romans – and was frequently portrayed as the divine hero Hercules, complete with lion skin and club. He also demanded worship as a living god.

Physically, Commodus was "of a striking appearance, with a shapely, manly body and a handsome face", according to Herodian, but the *Augustan Histories* describe him as having a drunkard's dullness of expression. After a serious fire damaged the city in AD191, Commodus decided to refound Rome as Colonia Commodiana (Colony of Commodus) on 1 January AD193. Such rampant megalomania led to a conspiracy among his closest courtiers. Eclectus, the imperial chamberlain, Quintus Laetus, the Praetorian prefect, and his favourite concubine, Marcia, together planned his assassination on 31 December AD192. Marcia gave him poison but he vomited it up, so a gladiator had to strangle him to death. The Senate then damned Commodus as "more cruel than Domitian, more foul than Nero", but four years later Septimius Severus deified him as part of his campaign to adopt himself retrospectively into the Antonine dynasty.

ELAGABALUS
(REIGNED AD218–22)

Born in Syria in AD204, Elagabalus was perhaps the most bizarre of all Rome's emperors. As a child he assumed the hereditary high priesthood of the Semitic sun god, taking its name, Elagabal. He was proclaimed emperor as Marcus Aurelius Antoninus Pius in May AD218 by a lover of his grandmother, Julia Maesa, sister-in-law of the former emperor Caracalla, who was still revered by the army. Elagabalus did not reach

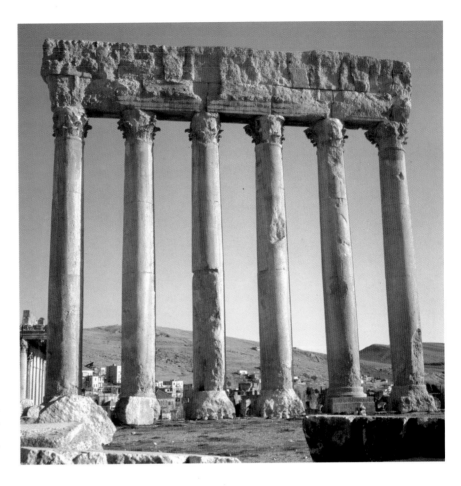

Rome until AD219, which he entered in company of a divine black stone that the Syrians claimed had fallen from heaven, walking backwards before its chariot, which was drawn by white horses. He installed this meteorite in a new temple on the Capitol and made it the supreme god of Rome, even above Jupiter. This was not a popular move, and the new god's often orgiastic worship, rumoured to include secret human sacrifice, principally of small children, alienated the city further, as did Elagabalus' marriage to one of the sacred Vestal Virgins. Elagabalus' almost pathological sex life perhaps indicates transexuality, for he used to prostitute himself to men in cheap bordellos and asked his doctors to cut an artificial vagina into his body. Such bizarreness completed his unpopularity. Only the semi-competent government of his mother and grandmother, and the prospect of his very different cousin Alexander Severus as successor, delayed his assassination until 11 March AD222.

Above: The temple of Jupiter Heliopolitanus in Baalbek in the province of Syria, from where the later Severans came.

Below: Elagabalus was only 14 when he came to the throne, but already depraved.

SAVIOURS OF THE EMPIRE

Above: Under Gallienus, the empire seemed to touch rock bottom. Then, largely due to his new ideas, it began its long, slow recovery, although he himself was soon murdered.

Below: The walls with which Aurelian hastily encircled Rome in the 270s incorporated existing older buildings such as the Claudian aqueduct.

With the murder of Alexander in AD235, the empire began to glide into chaos. Rival emperors formed separatist realms while, amid endless civil war, barbarian invaders penetrated deep into the empire. Most emperors were army men, acclaimed by greedy legionaries, then casually murdered. But a few, whose efforts helped save the empire in its darkest hours, stand out and deserve to be remembered as restorers of Rome.

GALLIENUS (AD253–68)

Although his reign saw chunks of the empire break away, Gallienus is now seen to have laid the foundations for its subsequent recovery and to have been a patron of the arts. On becoming co-emperor with his father, Valerian, in AD253, he took over the west while his father took the east. Valerian had initial successes against the Persian invaders in Syria, but he ended his life as a Persian captive. Gallienus was unable to revenge this because of barbarian invasions over the Danube. He repelled these but had to accept Postumus' separatist empire in Gaul and Spain. However, Gallienus rescinded his father's anti-Christian edicts and was a patron of the Neoplatonist philosopher Plotinus. He also encouraged a new style in sculpture that revived Augustan classicism, besides being a poet himself. His significant reforms, however, were military. He banned senators from army command and made Milan, closer to the threatened frontiers, capital in all but name, leaving Rome increasingly a ceremonial city. Finally, he created the empire's first armed reserve, a mobile force of crack troops called the *comitatus* (retinue). He also minted new coins to pay them in place of the debased currency. With this new model army, he crushed the Goths in AD268 at Nis in Serbia, killing 50,000, although he was assassinated soon after by his own troops.

AURELIAN (AD270–75)

Commander of Gallienus' new cavalry wing, and possibly involved in the plot against him, Aurelian was one of the Illyrian emperors, tough capable soldiers from the Romanized Balkans who helped save the empire. After turning back another German invasion in AD271, he decided to refortify Rome, three centuries after Augustus had removed most of the Servian walls. The new Aurelianic walls, still standing, ran for 12 miles (19km) and were rushed up, often incorporating older structures. After a victorious campaign against Zenobia of Palmyra in the east, he defeated the Gallic separatists at Châlons in AD274, reuniting the empire in just four years. Aurelian celebrated by building a huge temple in Rome to *Sol Invictus* (the Unconquered Sun), decorating it with booty from Palmyra's temples. Solar monotheism was popular with the army and he presumably hoped the new cult would help unify the empire. The next year, preparing to fight Persia, he was murdered by his secretary for unknown reasons and was mourned by both the army and the Senate.

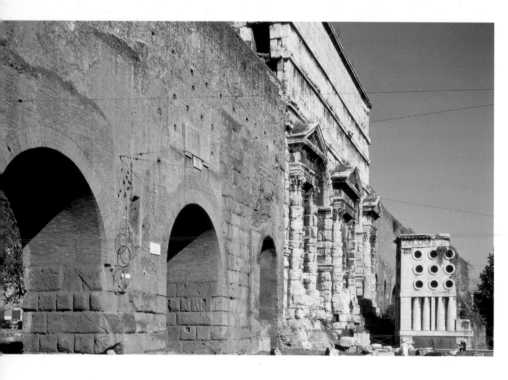

DIOCLETIAN (AD284–305)

Diocletian was one of the greatest of Rome's later emperors, recasting the empire in a bureaucratic, half-oriental mode that essentially lasted three centuries, an achievement for a man who remained, beneath his imperial splendour, a simple Illyrian soldier. Diocletian realized that the empire's crucial weakness lay in the fickle way the armies made and deposed emperors, and the lack of any principles for the succession. In AD286 he made his fellow soldier, Maximian, co-Augustus. They divided the empire, Diocletian taking the east, and both began campaigning energetically, if not always successfully. In AD293 Diocletian adopted Galerius as Caesar, his junior emperor and heir. Maximian did the same with Constantius I in the west. A Caesar was to succeed his Augustus in this Tetrarchy, or quadruple rulership. Each tetrarch adorned his administrative capital – Trier and Milan in the west, Thessalonica and Nicomedia (north Turkey) in the east – with palaces, basilicas and monuments. Each court's elaborate rituals were based on Persian models, elevating the emperor to semi-divine status to help guard against assassination. A two-tier administrative system was adopted. Provincial governors lost their military powers and their provinces were split and then grouped into 12 dioceses, or super-provinces. The army was expanded and reorganized along Gallienus' lines, with fixed frontier troops and *Palatini*, mobile forces directly under the emperor. The new system was successful; the Persians were defeated and the frontier extended further east in AD297, while Britain was restored to the empire by Constantius.

FINANCIAL REFORMS

This extra government came at a huge cost. Diocletian tried to make the tax burden more predictable and equitable, but was unable to check inflation. His notorious Edict of Maximum Prices in AD301, which fixed prices and wages, merely meant that goods disappeared from the markets, although workers were increasingly tied to their jobs like serfs. Nor was Diocletian's religious policy successful. Persecution of Christians, who were seen as unpatriotic blasphemers, even traitors, for their refusal to worship the gods of Rome, began in AD298 and became more savage in AD303. In the west, Maximian and Constantius hardly persecuted them, but in the more Christianized east, several thousands were martyred from AD303 to AD311 and many more abjured their faith. But in one area Diocletian was outstandingly successful: he died peacefully. In AD305, worn out, he abdicated – the first Roman emperor to do so – and retired to his vast fortified palace at Split in Dalmatia. He emerged only once, in AD308, to try to restore peace among his quarrelling successors, for the principles governing succession in the Tetrarchy did not work at all as intended. He died perhaps disappointed at the way his scheme was unravelling, but at least he died in his bed. His basic reforms underpinned the whole later empire.

Above: Under Diocletian, the empire entered a new, less chaotic phase marked by increasing bureaucratization and official attempts to control all aspects of life.

Below: Not least of Diocletian's achievements was being able to retire peacefully to his specially built palace at Split on the Adriatic, although his plans for the succession soon fell apart.

Above: Father of Constantine the Great, Constantius Chlorus was an effective ruler in his own right, regaining Britain for the empire and ruling it and Gaul wisely for many years as a Caesar, or junior emperor. He showed religious tolerance.

Right: Constantius received an enthusiastic welcome from Londoners after his troops reached the city in time to prevent its sack by the usurper Allectus' Frankish mercenaries.

CONSTANTIUS I, CAESAR (AD293–305), AUGUSTUS (AD305–06)

Constantius I, nicknamed "Chlorus", or pale – possibly from the leukemia that finally killed him – is often seen merely as the father of Constantine the Great. In fact, he was a successful ruler in his own right, most notably in his restoration of Britain to the empire. The Augustus Maximian's Praetorian prefect, he was made his heir and Caesar (junior emperor) in AD293, and made Trier his capital. He married Maximian's daughter Theodora, putting aside Helena, the mother of Constantine, who may not have been his legal wife. His first major task was to remove the separatist British empire of Carausius. He drove Carausius from Boulogne in AD293 and then invaded Britain in AD296. His troops reached London in time to stop Frankish mercenaries sacking it, which so pleased Londoners that they struck a medal hailing Constantius as the "restorer of light". A restoration of the whole province followed, ushering in a prosperous half century. Nine years later, Constantius, now a full Augustus, returned to Britain and led a campaign to crush the Picts, before returning to York to die of illness in July AD306. Constantius was notably tolerant in religious matters, ignoring the great persecution of Christians started by Galerius and Diocletian. He was a worshipper of *Sol Invictus* (the Unconquered Sun), a form of solar monotheism popular in the army at the time.

JULIAN "THE APOSTATE" (AD 361–3)

As a 24-year-old philosophy student in Athens, Julian had no political or military experience, being noted only for his inky fingers and his unfashionable beard, when his distant cousin Constantius II summoned him to rule the west as a Caesar in AD355. Julian had grown up partly in a remote castle in Cappadocia, where he studied the Greek classics and recoiled from the machinations of the court. Because the court was also avowedly Christian, Julian began to see all Christians as corrupt and murderous. Constantius, surviving son of Constantine – his two brothers had been murdered – could not deal both with a Gaul overrun by Germans and with the eastern frontier. To great surprise, Julian proved very successful as a general, repelling the Alamanni at Strasbourg in AD357 and marching across the Rhine, emulating Julius Caesar. Julian also reformed the administration, reducing some of the crushing taxes on civilians. Jealous, Constantius tried to recall him in AD360, but Julian's troops proclaimed him Augustus. Civil war was averted by Constantius II's death in AD361, when Julian became sole emperor. He now declared himself a pagan; he had long secretly worshipped the old gods. Although he never persecuted Christians, he forbade them to teach, hoping to reverse the rising Christian tide by excluding them from Greek culture, still overwhelmingly important for anyone with pretensions to learning. Julian himself wrote some philosophy and even a satire. Early in AD363 he invaded Persia with a huge army. He reached, but could not capture, its walled capital Ctesiphon (Baghdad). He then turned back for some reason and was killed, probably by a Christian in his army, on the retreat. His pagan restoration, like his several attempts at administrative reform, died with him, but religiously and militarily he had gained a few years more for Rome and her gods.

Above: The emperor Julian, bearded like ancient Greek philosophers, whose attempted pagan restoration died with him.

VALENTINIAN I
(AD364–75)

A man of the people, Valentinian was another Danubian soldier. He had risen through the ranks to become one of Julian's senior commanders, although the two had not got on well. Tall, fair-haired and blue-eyed, he had a commanding presence and a vigorous personality. Decently educated, he became perhaps the last great emperor in the west.

After the brief reign of the emperor Jovian, who died of natural causes, Valentinian was unanimously acclaimed emperor by the army and civil service in Constantinople. At once dividing the empire, he generously gave his younger brother Valens the east, which was by then much the richer half. He himself moved to Milan, and began to campaign vigorously against Germans who had crossed the Rhine. Driving them back, he marched up the Neckar valley and won a victory in the Black Forest. Then he moved north to Trier, which became once again the capital of the whole western

empire. This proved fortunate for Britain, suffering barbarian attacks. Valentinian sent Count Theodosius north in AD368 to restore order. Following an illness in AD367, Valentinian had raised his 8-year-old son Gratian to the throne with him. This was not an inspired choice. Gratian proved an ineffectual emperor, chiefly interested in religion. Valentinian was generally noted for being a poor judge of men, and for having a violent temper. The latter proved fatal. In AD375 he was in Pannonia to repel German invaders. Angered by the insolence of some German envoys, he died of a stroke. Valentinian was also noted for two things seldom associated with late-Roman emperors: a genuine compassion for the poor, whom he tried to help by extending the system of public health in Rome; and, despite his Christian faith, a religious tolerance that was becoming increasingly rare. Meanwhile, his brother Valens in the east was persecuting pagans, and also the Christian majority who did not agree with his version of Christianity, which denied the divinity of Christ. Valens led Rome's forces to a catastrophic defeat at the hands of the Goths at Adrianople in AD378, a defeat from which the empire never fully recovered.

Below: The base of the Egyptian obelisk in the hippodrome in Constantinople, the new eastern capital, shows the emperor Theodosius I receiving the submission of barbarian tribes. Theodosius spent most of his reign (AD379–95) fighting his numerous Roman rivals, but he was the last emperor to rule the whole empire.

CONSTANTINE THE GREAT

Above: Founder of the city of Constantinople and the first Christian Roman emperor, Constantine regarded himself as the "thirteenth apostle".

Below: Constantine was almost the last emperor to adorn Rome with edifices such as baths, a basilica and this triple arch.

Now famed for being the first Christian Roman emperor and for founding Constantinople as the "New Rome", later the capital of the eastern or Byzantine half of the empire, Constantine was, above all, a supremely competent general and a ruthlessly ambitious politician.

Like many other Roman emperors, Constantine's background was that of a soldier. Born *c.*AD276, his father was Constantius I, "Chlorus" (pale), one of Diocletian's junior emperors. Rumours that his mother was a prostitute can probably be dismissed, although Helena was not the saintly Romano-British noblewoman of legend. Constantine was serving with Diocletian's army when his father became Augustus in May AD305. Hastening across the empire, he joined Constantius in Britain.

On Constantius' death at York in AD306, his troops hailed his son as Augustus – prematurely, for at first he was only accepted as Caesar of the west and Constantine initially established his

Above: Emperor Constantine converted to Christianity late in life, yet his role as the founder of the Byzantine civilization is indisputable. Along with his mother Helena, he is still revered by Greek Orthodox Christians as a saint.

capital at Trier in Gaul. In the ensuing struggles, Constantine was victorious over Maxentius, ruler of Italy, at the Battle of the Milvian Bridge in AD312. He attributed his victory to a dream in which Christ had appeared telling him to mark his soldiers' shields with a cross (or so the story goes). Henceforth, Constantine's soldiers always fought under the cross – at least according to Eusebius, an almost contemporary Christian writer anxious to portray Constantine as a true Christian.

In AD313 Constantine, now Augustus of the west, declared religious tolerance for Christians and pagans alike, although he was already moving towards Christianity. In AD324, when he became sole ruler of the empire, he forbade public sacrifices and ritual prostitution and looted pagan temples to finance his church-building programme, which included the first basilica of St Peter's in Rome. He also presided over the Council of Nicaea (Iznik) in AD325, in vain trying to promote religious unity before finally agreeing to persecute those declared heretics by the Council.

Although Constantine's conversion was almost certainly genuine – he saw himself as the "thirteenth apostle" – religious conviction was also much reinforced by political convenience: the Church's highly effective social organization impressed him, as did the prospect of despoiling pagan temple treasures.

DIOCLETIAN'S HEIR

A revolutionary in religion, Constantine continued with Diocletian's army reforms and further elaborated court ritual, wearing a bejewelled diadem and, allegedly, in later years a wig. If personal vanity was a failing, so was paranoia, for he had his son Crispus by his first wife executed for adultery in AD326. Rumours that the current empress Faustina had intrigued against her stepson – either to advance her own sons or because Crispus had rejected her advances – seemed born out by her suicide soon after, when the emperor's mother, Helena, convinced Constantine of Faustina's guilt. (In the new, ever more elaborate "Byzantine" court, eunuchs played an increasingly vital role as major officials. They appealed to absolutist rulers because they could never found rival dynasties themselves.)

Constantine minted the first *solidus* coin, which, at 72 to the pound (454g) of gold, provided a stable gold currency for many centuries, although inflation continued. Otherwise, his financial policies burdened civilians even more heavily. A new tax, the *chrysagryon*, payable in gold or silver, was levied every four years on citizens. It was so onerous that fathers allegedly sold their daughters to pay it, but money was needed for the huge court, army and building programme. Constantine completed Maxentius' gigantic Basilica Nova in Rome and constructed his own arch – plundering other arches for its decoration. He also built the Baths of Constantine, the ancient city's last grand building, and a palace for the pope. But Constantine did not find Rome, with its proudly pagan memories, sympathetic.

CONSTANTINOPOLI

CONSTANTINOPLE

Byzantium had been a small Greek city for almost 1,100 years when it was chosen as Constantine's new capital in AD324. Easy to defend and superbly sited between Europe and Asia, this New Rome, or Constantinople (Istanbul), became a great city. It was later given a Roman-style Senate and its citizens received handouts of free grain and circuses. Constantine liberally adorned his new capital with artworks taken from Greek cities and built new palaces, fora and churches, as well as temples dedicated to Jupiter, Juno and Minerva, echoing those of Rome.

The Byzantine civilization was a fusion of Greek, Roman and the emerging Christian tradition. For this achievement alone, Constantine deserves the title "Great". When he died in May AD337, he was buried in the Church of the Holy Apostles in Constantinople. However, the Senate in Rome deified a ruler who had not resigned the old pagan title of *pontifex maximus*, higher priest, held by every emperor since Augustus. Such a contradiction demonstrates Constantine stood halfway between the old pagan empire of Rome and the deeply Christian Byzantine empire that replaced it and which lasted another eleven centuries.

Above: One of Constantine's greatest feats was the founding of Constantinople. For over a millennium it was one of the greatest cities on earth.

Below: Constantine was a fine general. This ivory shows him triumphing over his enemies.

WOMEN BEHIND THE THRONE

Although women in Rome could never hold office or vote, by the late Republic they could own, manage and inherit property. They also joined men at dinner parties and shared Rome's political and cultural life. If their men were of high status, women could also aspire to become powers behind the throne, even occasionally becoming effective rulers.

LIVIA DRUSILLA (59BC–AD29)

In 38BC Livia Drusilla became Augustus' third wife, having divorced her first husband, Tiberius Claudius, by whom she had had two sons: Tiberius and Drusus. As she and Augustus had no children, Augustus adopted first his nephew Marcellus, then his grandsons Gaius and Lucius as his heirs, and only last, when the others had died, Livia's son Tiberius. Because of this, she was suspected of procuring their deaths, although this may be unjust – mortality rates were high at the time – and is certainly unprovable. We do know that Livia gave Augustus invaluable support and stability. The clemency he showed to his (few) enemies in later life was said to stem from her advice. She also tolerated his frequent infidelities, even when he left for Gaul in 16BC accompanied by Terentia, his then mistress. When Tiberius succeeded Augustus in AD14, Livia was rumoured to have poisoned him and his last surviving grandson, Agrippa Postumus. But it is probable that Agrippa, excluded from the succession for psychopathic tendencies, was killed by Tiberius. Livia died at the age of 88, a Julio-Claudian matriarch.

JULIA AGRIPPINA

A sister of Caligula and great-granddaughter of Augustus, Julia Agrippina had married Domitius Ahenobarbus, a greatnephew of Augustus, which made their son Nero doubly descended from the first emperor. Once divorced from Domitius, Agrippina married her uncle, Claudius, in AD49, who had had his third wife, Messalina, executed for plotting against him.

Agrippina plotted to have Nero succeed in place of Britannicus, Claudius' son by Messalina. In AD51 Nero became *princeps iuventutis* (leader of youth), with Seneca, his tutor, and Burrus, one of Agrippina's protégés, head of the Praetorian guard. All was ready for Nero's succession when Agrippina (probably) had Claudius poisoned in October AD54. Britannicus was executed and she hoped to rule through the 17-year-old Nero. At first he showed her respect, but in AD55 she was expelled from the palace and exiled. In AD59 Nero tried to murder her by having a specially built ship sink under her. However, she swam to shore and it took a freed man of Nero's called Anicetus to finish her off. So perished "the best of mothers", as Nero had once called her.

JULIA MAMMAEA

When Alexander Severus succeeded his assassinated cousin, the depraved Elagabalus, to become emperor in AD222, he was only 14 years old and under the sway of his mother, the Syrian princess Julia Mammaea. He never managed to

Above: Mother of the emperor Nero and last wife of the ageing Claudius, Agrippina aspired to rule through both. But although she (probably) murdered Claudius, her son soon tired of her and had her killed in turn.

Below: Livia, wife of Augustus and mother of Tiberius, had great influence if not power while her husband lived. But after Augustus' death during the grape harvest, Tiberius increasingly ignored her.

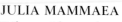

escape her maternal domination, but at first Julia ruled very effectively. She reversed all Elegabalus' scandalous policies, chose 16 distinguished senators as advisers and relied heavily on the famous lawyer Ulpian, also from Syria, whom she made commander of the Praetorians. However, Ulpian proved unable to control the Praetorians, and was finally murdered by them in AD228.

Meanwhile, Julia had become madly jealous of her son's wife, Barbia Orbiana, whom Alexander had married in AD225, and whose father he had made Caesar or co-ruler. Julia had her daughter-in-law thrown out of the palace and her father executed. Being still dominated by his mother, Alexander accepted this, but Julia could not control foreign attacks. After an inconclusive expedition to repel a Persian invasion in AD232, mother and son went north to deal with a German attack. Alexander so alienated the Rhine legions by his military feebleness and his meanness about their pay that they chose the giant Maximinus as emperor in AD235. Troops sent to kill Alexander found him clinging to his mother in a tent. Mother and son were butchered together, so ending the Severan dynasty.

GALLA PLACIDIA (AD392–50)

Daughter of Theodosius I the Great, grand-daughter of Valentinian I and half-sister of the emperor Honorius (one of the feeblest emperors), Placidia herself was a far stronger character than her half-brother. However, her efforts to preserve the empire foundered partly on her own likes and dislikes. Abducted by the invading Visigoths in AD410, she was carried off to Gaul and forcibly married to the Visigoth king, Ataulf. She owed her return to Italy to Constantius III, a general who took control of the western empire in AD413 and forced the Visigoths to settle around Toulouse. In AD417 he married Placidia against her wishes. However, his death in late AD421 left their infant son the official emperor: Valentinian III (AD425–55).

After a brief interregnum, troops from Constantinople helped Placidia to gain control of Ravenna, the new imperial capital, and she began ruling through her son, Valentinian, trying to maintain imperial power amid the gathering chaos. She had to rely, however, on the armies of the general Aetius, a highly effective soldier whom she for some reason came to loathe. She embroiled him in a dispute with Boniface, governor of North Africa, that had terrible consequences. Boniface enlisted the support of the Vandals, a German tribe who had settled in southern Spain. This was disastrous, for after their entry into Africa in AD429 they were never dislodged. In AD439 they captured Carthage, cutting off Rome's grain supply. Aetius proved more successful in Europe, defeating the Huns in AD451 at Châlons. By then Placidia was dead. She did not live to see the end of her dynasty, for Valentinian proved fatally incompetent. Jealous of Aetius, he had him murdered before being killed himself by two of Aetius' officers in AD455, leaving no heirs. Shortly afterwards, the Vandals landed near Rome and sacked it, carrying off Valentinian's widow and thousands of Romans. The empire soon ceased to exist.

Above: The ruins of Baalbek (Heliopolis) in Syria, the home province of Julia Mammaea, who in reality governed the empire for 13 years during the reign of her ineffectual young son, Alexander Severus.

Above: Daughter of emperor Theodosius, Galla Placidia was far more determined than her half-brother, the emperor Honorius, but she was too often swayed by her personal feelings to pursue effective imperial policies and actually hastened the empire's fall.

CHAPTER IV

GOVERNING THE EMPIRE

Seeing Rome for the first time in 166BC, the Greek historian Polybius was struck by the apparent excellence of its government, thinking it combined the best aspects of democracy in its Assembly of the people, of aristocracy, embodied in the Senate, and monarchy, in its elected officials or consuls. This seemingly perfect system of checks and balances made Rome's status as ruler of the Mediterranean world look well deserved.

But during the Republic and Principate, Rome never had a written constitution. Real power lay in the informal network of alliances and *clientalia*, the web of dependants that each Roman noble needed for a political career. The Senate, dominated by the interests of its noble elite, failed to cope with the problems of governing an expanding empire. This led to the Republic's downfall and its replacement by the emperors. Under imperial rule, the Senate became increasingly ceremonial and the Assembly disappeared, while the provinces rivalled Rome in power and privilege, if never in prestige. By the 4th century AD, the Roman empire had become an absolute monarchy, albeit one where the emperor (at least in theory) obeyed the laws. The full codification of laws by Justinian in the 6th century AD meant that the Roman legacy transmitted to the Middle Ages was more autocratic than democratic, an inspiration more to rulers than the ruled.

Left: At the very heart of Roman life and of the whole empire lay the Forum Romanum, adorned with monuments such as the triple triumphal arch erected by Septimius Severus.

A SELF-GOVERNING CONFEDERACY

Above: The Maison Carrée at Nîmes, France, one of the finest temples of the Augustan era, testifies to the prosperous sophistication of such colonies founded by Rome but growing into confidently self-governing cities that contributed to the empire's strength.

Below: Ostia, at the mouth of the Tiber, was Rome's first colony, the forerunner of many hundreds planted around the Mediterranean and Europe. Later its nearby port became Rome's greatest harbour, supplying the voracious capital.

Rome ruled its growing empire with the minimum of government by co-opting the aristocracies of other cities, first in Italy then around the Mediterranean, into ruling on Rome's behalf. In essence, the empire became a confederation of internally self-governing cities. Defence and foreign affairs were transferred to Rome's control, however. Unlike other ancient cities with empires, notably Athens, Rome was generous in granting citizenship to other towns in Italy. As its empire spread to the less urbanized parts of Europe, it planted colonies of Roman citizens or made existing cities into Roman colonies, so that the empire ended up as an agglomerate of more than 1,000 cities. (New cities without this status were founded as well.) Urbanization helped spread Roman culture around the empire.

In 381BC the Romans seized Tusculum, a Latin city, and part of the Latin League of cities around Rome. All its citizens were granted Roman citizenship, which they happily accepted, later supplying many consuls. But there were limits to granting full citizenship, if existing Roman citizens were not to be outnumbered. Another type of citizenship, *civitas sine suffragio*, came with all rights except the franchise, and was imposed on cities of the Latin League after their defeat in 338BC. These cities retained internal autonomy, electing their own magistrates, who often got full citizenship. They had to supply troops to Rome when required, serving under their own officers. If they settled in Rome, they became Roman citizens. This halfway house to full citizenship long satisfied the Latin cities.

Rome now began founding colonies of self-governing settlements, both Latin colonies of mixed Latins and Romans, such as Calvi near Capua, and wholly Roman ones, such as Ostia in *c*.350BC. Between 343 and 264BC, about 60,000 colonists received allotments of land in some 40 colonies throughout Italy, from Cremona to Brindisi. Peoples of Italy not thought worthy of Latin citizenship, such as the rough Samnites, were made *socii*, allies, bound to Rome by bilateral treaties. They lost control of their foreign policy and had to supply troops but retained autonomy. The effectiveness of this system was revealed in the cities' loyalty during the Punic wars, when Rome looked doomed. A century later, Italians pressed for full citizenship. The war of the Allies, the Social War, gained full citizenship for all Latins and Italians in 89BC.

COLONIES OVERSEAS

Among the more radical proposals of Gaius Gracchus was the founding of a colony overseas for some of Rome's landless citizens on the site of Carthage, destroyed 23 years earlier. This proposal came to nothing, as did a similar idea for overseas colonies by Saturninus, a Marian tribune, in 102BC. Only under Caesar was the planting of colonies of Romans resumed, mostly for retired legionaries, but his plans included settling 80,000 unemployed Romans abroad. Arles, Tarragona, Fréjus, plus Carthage and

Corinth rising from their ruins, were among his foundations. Under Augustus, who had even more veterans to settle, colonies of ex-legionaries were founded at Turin, Avignon, Nîmes, Cologne and Zaragossa, among others. All have flourished ever since, showing that Augustus and his legates, like Caesar before him, had a good eye for cities. These colonies were self-governing cities with Roman rights, and include Timgad in Algeria, founded by Trajan for his veterans, and Camulodunum (Colchester), founded by Claudius as capital of Britain.

In the east, an old Hellenistic city such as Tarsus might win Roman rights for some (including St Paul), but it was in the west that Roman colonization really bore fruit. Places like Vienne and Lyons acquired Roman rights and grew into fine cities, with theatres, baths and forums. A grade lower were *municipia* with Latin rights, whose magistrates became full Roman citizens. Below them were *civitates*, urban settlements. The tendency was to upgrade any city that proved worthy. London started as a mere *civitas*, but became a *colonia* and the provincial capital.

Above: The Temple of the Spirit of the Colony at Timgad in Algeria, a colony for veteran legionaries founded by the emperor Trajan.

THE OLIGARCHICAL REPUBLIC

Above: This bronze dating from the 5th century BC supposedly portrays Brutus, one of the nobles who helped – according to legend – to expel the last Etruscan king, Tarquin.

The three-fold constitution that Polybius so admired – the people, gathered in the *comitia*, or Assembly; the Senate, or Council of Elders, composed of older nobles; and the magistrates themselves, annual officials elected by the *comitia* – had existed in that form since only 287BC, although parts of it may have predated the expulsion of the kings in 509BC. Certainly the Senate itself went back at least to the 6th century BC.

In theory, the people, as constituted in the *comitia*, or Assembly, were sovereign and had unlimited powers. In practice, they met only when summoned by magistrates and could vote, without discussion, only on measures put before them. These restrictions meant that Rome was never a democracy in the sense that many Greek cities were in the classical age (480–322BC). This did not seem to concern the people, for they usually had little desire to guide the state. Their main interest was to be protected from any unjust or arbitrary actions by magistrates and nobles and to gain redress for their economic and legal grievances. Later in the Republic, when Rome had an empire to exploit, they also expected entertainment in the form of free, or very cheap, public games and grain – the so-called *panem et circenses* (bread and circuses). This aspect of Roman life survived the end of the Republic and was transplanted to Constantinople in AD330.

The *comitia centuriata*, or Assembly, was traditionally created by the kings, and continued into the Principate. Its origins were military (the kings wanted to establish an army based on heavy infantry), and it was structured corresponding to army divisions. The citizenry was divided into five classes and each class was subdivided into varying numbers of centuries, except the lowest or poorest class, which was exempt from military service. From the start, the Assembly was heavily weighted in favour of the richer citizens, for the more affluent centuries outnumbered the poorer ones in voting power, if not in numbers. As voting on every proposal started with the richer centuries and ended when an overall majority of centuries had voted, the poorest often did not vote at all. This was a long way from a one-man, one-vote democracy.

The Conflict of the Orders, or Class War, which lasted intermittently from 494 to 287BC, was about this democratic deficit and also economic problems. In the 5th century BC Rome suffered economically, partly due to the reduction in trade at the end of the monarchy, partly because of land shortages and partly because endless wars made it difficult for

Right: The Romans were intensely conscious of their ancestors. They kept their busts in their houses and at times they would parade solemnly with them in public. This statue dates from the 1st century BC.

the citizen-soldier, often fighting during the summer, to tend his farm properly. Many poorer citizens grew so heavily indebted that they became serfs, or *nexi*, of their creditors. Because of problems of this sort they threatened to secede – traditionally five times; the first in 494BC, when they gained new tribunes of the people, magistrates outside the senate-dominated run of offices who could veto measures on their behalf. The writing down of the Twelve Tables of the Law in 450BC was meant to help, but it took a range of measures, culminating in the *Lex Hortensia* of 287BC, by which the decrees of the *concilium plebis*, Council of the People, were to be binding on the whole state, for the conflict finally to be settled.

This did not mean that Rome had become in any way democratic, however, for richer citizens generally dominated the *concilium plebis* too, while the eminent plebeians who had, by law, been elected as one of the two consuls since 367BC, formed the so-called plebeian nobility. Further, the tribunes, once the people's defenders and leaders, were now increasingly co-opted into the Senate, first just to listen to debates but finally to initiate them. The tribunes, who were normally among the richer and therefore often the more ambitious of plebeians, thus joined the plebeian nobility, allied to the Senate rather than opposed to it, and the tribunate increasingly became just one office among others. If former tribunes began entering the Senate themselves, this reduced their effectiveness as champions of the poor, but it made for a welcome amity and unity in a state facing horrendous external threats. Under the emperors, the people finally lost their right to choose magistrates in AD14, and the *comitia* became a mere rubber stamp on the Senate's and emperor's decisions. But the informal powers of the people of Rome long remained a major force in Roman politics. Their approval, most vocally expressed in the amphitheatre or circus, was courted for as long as Rome remained the real capital.

THE MAGISTRATES

With Sulla's reforms in 82BC the *cursus honorum*, or ladder of office, was finalized, but before that the Roman system was oddly informal. The highest magistrates were always the two consuls, elected annually by the Assembly. They each had equal powers and could veto the other's, but this rarely happened. No one could (legally) be consul in successive years. In theory, no one under the age of 42 could become consul, but this check on youthful ambition was unsuccessful. Beneath the consuls were the praetors, whose numbers were steadily increased to eight under Sulla and under Caesar to 16. One praetor supervised the administration of justice, while another praetor dealt with foreigners. Propraetors, like the proconsuls, governed provinces after their year's office. To assist consuls there were quaestors, the most junior rank on the *cursus honorum*, and there were also two censors, elected every five years, who took a census of every citizen's wealth, including senators', demoting or promoting citizens. There were also four aediles who looked after the city's policing.

As the astute, if notably reactionary, senator Cato the Censor (234–149BC) justly observed, the Roman Republic was "not made by any one man, but by many; not in a single lifetime but over many centuries". Considering the overlapping of duties and powers, the Roman Republic worked remarkably well until its last century. But what made it work and lay behind the often fleeting powers of the magistrates and the often inchoate desires of the Assembly was the immense and enduring prestige of the Senate.

Below: Aulus Metellus, an orator of the late Republic (c.90BC), here declaims with a gesture typical of Roman public speaking. Rhetoric was always vital to Roman public life, essential not only for aspiring politicians but also lawyers and ordinary citizens.

ROME'S RULING CLASSES

Under the emperors, Rome was administered by its two upper classes, the Senate and the equestrians (knights). Although the Senate was older and more distinguished, equestrians came to play an increasingly crucial role in the state. The Roman people lost all political power.

THE SENATE

Unlike the senior house of modern republics, the Senate in Rome was not the upper house, for there was no lower house, only the Assembly. Nor was the Senate directly elected. However, as it consisted of men who had once been magistrates – elected by the Assembly – there was a democratic element in it

Below: The Curia (Senate House) seen through the ruins of the Temple of Saturn in the Forum Romanum. The present structure, surprisingly small, dates from the 4th century AD, and was rebuilt after a fire.

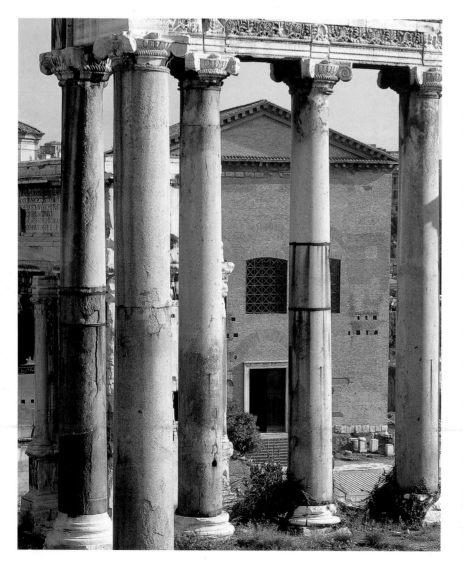

under the Republic. Traditionally, the city's founder, Romulus, chose 100 senior heads of important families as a royal council or Senate. Roman conservatism ensured that this ancient body survived not only the end of the Republic but even the passing of the emperors themselves. The Senate was still debating in the 6th century AD under the Ostrogoths.

The Senate of the early Republic was composed of 300 *patres familias*, or heads of households. They were joined by other prominent men, known as *patricii*, to form a proud nobility of about 1,000 families. From the 4th century BC, plebeian (new) nobles entered the Senate, intermarrying with the older nobility.

Magistrates in the Republic entered the Senate after a year in office as quaestor, the lowest rank. Unless the censors decided to the contrary, they held their seats for life. The Senate's formal powers – to preselect who could stand as magistrates, to approve measures before they went to the Assembly, to advise and consult – made it powerful enough, but this was eclipsed by its informal *auctoritas* (prestige, authority). The Senate expounded its views in a *senatus consultum*, the report of a debate. This had no legal authority, but magistrates normally accepted it. A late development was the *senatus consultum ultimum*, a decree to end all debate.

The Senate guided the Republic effectively through the Punic and later wars. When Hannibal camped outside Rome in 213BC, the Senate's *sang froid* helped save Rome. At that time its members were still recruited from an almost closed circle of *c.*2,000 men. Although they disagreed at times, they did not form destructively divisive factions. But by the time of the reformist Gracchi brothers (133–121BC), the consensus was breaking down and disputes led to violence and murder. From then on, the Senate's control of the state began to weaken. The coups and counter-coups of the 80s BC revealed that the Senate no longer controlled the generals. Despite Sulla's attempts to limit the latter's powers, the Senate lost control of Rome.

THE SENATE AND THE EMPERORS

Augustus tried to restore the Senate's dignity in running the empire. He held real power, but the Senate retained, and sometimes gained, important duties, including presiding over law courts and choosing governors for about a third of the provinces. Senators also continued to be appointed legates – meaning they held power delegated from the emperor – as governors of "imperial" provinces such as Gaul and as generals of legions. By AD 100 almost half the Senate was composed of provincials – citizens born outside Italy – and most consuls were not Italian born.

Senate-respecting rulers such as Trajan were balanced by despots such as Caligula or Domitian. Hadrian, a humane emperor, soured his relations with the Senate because he executed several members. The Senate sustained a nostalgia for Republican government long after this was remotely practicable. Augustus was punctilious in attending senatorial debates, but few of the later emperors paid it such attention. They were often too busy to do so.

SENATORIAL ORDER

To become a senator was to attain the highest honours in the state, except that of emperor. To win entry into the Senate, its members had to have a fortune in property (not cash) of one million sesterces. Many had far more. In practice, Senate membership in the Principate was mainly hereditary. The son of a senator started his career at the age of 20 as a military tribune and could enter the Senate as a quaestor at the age of 25 if chosen by the *princeps*. He then worked his way up the *cursus honorum* until, if he was lucky, becoming consul at the age of 43. Under the empire, a consul did not hold his office for a whole year but retired to let another fill the post. None of the offices carried a salary, but the governorship of a major province such as Africa did (one million sesterces a year), making it a coveted post.

Senators formed a class above normal Romans. They wore a special toga, which had a broad purple stripe, had the best seats at the theatre reserved for them and were often promised by a new emperor that their members would not be summarily arrested and executed. Until Diocletian, senatorial estates in Italy were free of tax, and even later senators retained many privileges, remaining immensely wealthy.

Above: The ancient Rostra (literally, ships' prows), from which magistrates made speeches in the Forum, Rome.

Below: Roman senators taking part in a procession for a consul's assumption of office c.270AD. Although by that date the Senate had lost almost all its political powers, it nevertheless retained immense prestige and wealth.

Above: While the equestrians as an order failed to maintain their distinctive status in the later empire, senators such as this 5th-century noble retained their importance and their regular meetings in the Senate House well into the 6th century.

Below: Head of a priest of Aphrodite, dating to the 1st century BC. Many of these local cults flourished under the Roman Empire, sometimes attracting the attention of senators from Rome.

THE EQUESTRIANS

Immediately beneath senators in prestige and dignity, and sometimes individually richer, were the equestrians, or knights. Originally, they had supplied the cavalry for the armies of the early Republic, being those relatively few citizens rich enough to equip themselves as horsemen. By 200BC they had lost this role to auxiliary cavalry. Excluded entirely from the *cursus honorum* of the senatorial nobility, they turned instead to making money. The big advantage they had over senators was that they were not barred from all forms of business. As the empire expanded south and east in the 3rd and 2nd centuries BC, literally golden opportunities arose for equestrians in banking, commerce, tax-collecting and bidding for the many government contracts – building bridges and harbours, supplying armies – that were farmed out. Most profitable of all was tax-farming. When the radical tribune Gaius Gracchus, presumably heedless of longer-term consequences, granted the equestrians the tax-collecting contracts for the Asian provinces in 122BC, he was rewarding his immediate political allies. But he also vastly boosted a powerful new class of businessmen who soon began to challenge the Senate's monopoly of office and power, and generally supported the *popularis* reformist party. Sulla, a keen *optimate*, or senatorial reactionary, proscribed (killed) 1,600 equestrians – compared to only 40 senators – when he tried to re-establish senatorial supremacy, but even he was forced to recruit from equestrian ranks for his much-enlarged Senate. Equestrians and their tax-collecting agents, the *publicani*, were among those massacred by angry Greeks in Delos and the cities of the Aegean in 88BC at the instigation of Mithradates.

Caesar made frequent use of equestrians, using them both to fill the Senate and as administrators, some of them being non-Italian multi-millionaires such as Lucius Balbus of Cadiz. By then, equestrians were numerous – there were 500 men of equestrian status in both Padua and Cadiz in Augustus' time. They provided a perfect source of enterprising, often enthusiastic men to run the empire under the Principate, for they had no senatorial-type nostalgia for the days of the Republic. Augustus employed equestrians widely, either as procurators or financial secretaries in charge of the finances of imperial provinces who could control the senatorial legate, or else as governors of those provinces such as Egypt where he wanted to exclude the Senate. In Rome he revived the annual mounted processions of equestrians that took place on 15 July, when up to 5,000 of them would ride past on their ceremonial horses. Tiberius' chief minister Sejanus was an equestrian – but he overstepped the mark, for

CURSUS HONORUM

Originally very flexible, this official career ladder or succession of magistracies was codified by the *Lex Villia Annalis* of 180BC and confirmed a century later by Sulla. After an initial ten years' military service and his 30th birthday, a well-connected Roman could hope to be elected one of the 20 quaestors, whose duties were chiefly financial. A quaestor automatically became a member of the Senate and might then hope to become an aedile. By the age of 38 he might be elected praetor and only at the age of 43 (39 before Sulla's reforms in 81BC) could he stand for the consulship. After being consul, he could become a governor of a province as a proconsul or perhaps a censor, one of two magistrates elected every five years to conduct a census of the Roman people, classifying them according to wealth and conduct. No office could in theory be held until at least two years had elapsed since his previous term of office. The aim, which failed disastrously in the end, was to stop men such as Marius, Pompey or Caesar becoming too powerful.

Tiberius, proudly conscious of his descent from the great Claudian family, struck Sejanus down.

To rank as an equestrian required a fortune of 300,000 sesterces, less than a third of a senator's. Equestrians could be recognized by the narrow purple stripes on their togas; they wore a special gold ring and had the second best seats in the theatres. To belong to the equestrian order did not require residence in Rome, unlike the Senate, and many in fact lived outside the city, either in Italy or in the provinces, often respected members and patrons of the local city magistracy. The sons of equestrians, though not automatically admitted to the order, in practice usually were, first serving as army officers, often in unglamorous posts such as remote frontier forts, then in civilian posts such as customs, finance and general administration. The leading treasury officials under the Principate were most often equestrians, as were the very highest posts in the empire: the prefectures of the corn supply, the *annona*; of the fleet; of the *vigiles*, the night watchmen/firemen; and last and most powerful, the Praetorian prefect, head of the Praetorian guard. Salaries for these posts were considerable, coming in grades of 60,000, 100,000 and 200,000 sesterces. Freedmen and centurions were sometimes given equestrian status and could hope to rise meritocratically. Hadrian (AD117–38) made extensive use of such new equestrians. Unlike senators, however, they had no *curia* (Senate house) as a focus for their class, and their name and status did not survive the end of the empire.

Below: Typical of the new business opportunities for the equestrians, who were allowed to take part in commerce, was the free port at Delos in Greece, which became the busiest entrepôt in the late Republic. Reputedly, Delos could handle the sale of up to 40,000 slaves a day.

THE SECRET WORKINGS OF ROMAN POLITICS

The oligarchic reality of the Republic, which negated its seemingly democratic constitution, depended on the huge web of patronage called *clientalia*. This was an informal, but openly acknowledged, system by which each noble commanded the loyalties of hundreds, or even thousands, of retainers bound to him in reciprocal relationship. This enabled the nobility to manipulate the Assembly, which otherwise could have shown signs of democratic independence. The tenacious network survived the end of the Republic, although it was the emperors who became its ultimate beneficiaries.

As early as the 5th century BC, possibly even under the kings, *clientalia* was an important part of Roman life. At its simplest, it was a personal relationship of mutual obligation between the *patronus*, the patron, who was generally a great aristocrat or patrician, and his *clientes*, or dependants, humble and usually impoverished plebeians. In the Republic's later years, such clients came to include freedmen, usually former slaves of the *patronus*, who formed an increasingly numerous group. But unless these freedmen became Roman citizens – and so able to vote – they were second-class *clientes*. Only a full Roman citizen could expect to receive the *sportula*, regular little presents in cash or kind that a client expected from his patron.

The patron would look after his clients in many aspects of life – if they went to law, needed to borrow money, needed advice in general or a guardian for their children. In return, a client gave his patron political support, both by voting for him and his allies in the Assembly and also by augmenting his personal following. The patron saw himself as a *paterfamilias* in relation to his clients, as head of an extended family, and their relationship had the same sort of highly charged feelings of *pietas* (piety) and *fides* (faithfulness) expected in a family.

For the ordinary Roman in a city grown impersonally vast, being a client offered certain advantages besides the obvious financial and legal help a great man could give. It gave a client a feeling of belonging and participating in the affairs of one of the great families who ran the growing empire. By 200BC the major noble families were organizing their bands of *clientes* on a professional basis, mobilizing them in great blocks to vote as required, and to cajole and threaten other voters when required. Tiberius and

Below: Most of public life, not just political, but also social and legal, took place in the Forum Romanum. Here too the networks of clients and patrons could be renewed, cemented or extended.

Gaius Gracchus were murdered by clients of the optimate senators, not by the senators themselves. The system continued in an apolitical way even after Tiberius had removed the Assembly's last political powers of electing magistrates.

The concept of *clientalia* spilt over into Rome's dealings with its allies and subjects. When Quintus Flaminius declared "freedom" for the Greek cities in 196BC, the sort of relationship he saw between the Greeks and Rome was not total independence but the symbiotic client–patron relationship that worked so well in Rome. The Greeks did not see it this way, having known real freedom, and it took brutal repression by Rome before they accepted the new status quo. But later, when Rome extended its power east to less liberty-addicted kingdoms in western Asia, this informal, essentially personal, system worked well.

MILITARY *CLIENTALIA*
The army was for a long time outside the client system, as of all political life – armies were not allowed into Italy and weapons could not be carried openly in Rome. But from the time of Marius' reforms in 106–102BC, soldiers, now recruited even from the poorest classes, began looking to their generals for rewards for their loyalty in exactly the

same way that civilian clients did. The results proved disastrous for the Republic. Caesar's army also formed part of his *clientalia*, as, in a different way, did all his supporters, most of them definitely new men – equestrians or men from the Italian municipal aristocracies or people from even further afield.

Octavian went even further. Preparing for the war with Antony, the climax of his struggle for supremacy, in 32BC, Octavian pressed all the leading men throughout Italy – not just the senators and equestrians in Rome but the local aristocracy of the *municipia* – to swear an oath to him. *"Tota Italia in mea verba iuravit"* (All Italy swore an oath of loyalty to me) he later recorded in the *Res Augustae*, which list his accomplishments. Having sworn such an oath, these men, the ruling classes in the widest sense, became in effect his clients, bound to him by ties of reciprocal fealty. When soldiers swore loyalty to the *princeps* as their supreme commander – although Octavian was never much of a general – the armies, too, effectively became his clients. This personal tie underpinned the Principate throughout its existence; many civilian client–patron relationships had long been hereditary. For the Principate as much as the Republic, therefore, *clientalia* acted as a sort of invisible glue.

Above: As princeps, *or the leading citizen of the state, Augustus was the greatest patron of them all – a role he extended into military life, also binding the army to him.*

Below: Life in the insulae, *the often cramped apartment blocks where most Romans lived, could be grim. Being the client of a rich patron offered a small chance of improvement or at least some support.*

THE PRINCIPATE
A MONARCHY IN DISGUISE

Above: The arrival of Vespasian in Rome in AD69 marked the advent of the second dynasty of emperors: the Flavians. Shorter-lived than the Julio-Claudians, this era ended when Domitian, the last of the Flavians, was assassinated in AD96.

Below: The dramatic public murder of Julius Caesar in 44BC was a stark warning to later emperors to exercise their (unofficial) power with greater discretion and tact. Many failed to do so – and paid the inevitable price.

In February 44BC Caesar, victor of the civil war, had himself created perpetual dictator. Partly because of this latest, most blatant, addition to his powers, he was assassinated soon after. Octavian, later Augustus, was wiser, disguising the absolutist foundations of his new regime so carefully that the Senate could go along with his restoration of the Republic – meaning a stable constitutional government, not rule by the "Senate and People of Rome". Gradually the emperor appeared more and more as an autocrat, whose power depended on force. In the turmoil of the 3rd century AD, the trappings of absolutism finally emerged until, under Diocletian and Constantine, the emperor became a superhuman being, surrounded by genuflecting courtiers.

"If Caesar with all his genius could not find a way out [of the crisis], who can possibly do so?" Gaius Matius, one of Caesar's followers, asked Cicero in a letter soon after Caesar's assassination. It took two more rounds of civil wars before Augustus found an answer. His Second Settlement of 23BC meant that he no longer monopolized the consulate, but let other members of the Senate hold this much-desired office. In fact, it became customary for the first consul of the year to make way for a second. Augustus did his utmost to restore the forms of the Republic – he was ostentatiously first among equals, the *princeps* – and to breathe new if restricted life into its institutions. He offered the senatorial nobility careers running the empire, army and Rome itself. Although Augustus' own household, along with his public behaviour, was notably modest – in reality his wealth, like his power, was vast.

Augustus' successors lacked the tact, patience and *auctoritas* to dissemble so successfully. Tiberius, the next emperor and in many ways deeply traditional, unwittingly revealed the real nature of the Principate by making Sejanus his effective prime minister, although Sejanus was a knight, not a senator, disqualified for high office. Tiberius withdrew to Capri for the last decade of his life and ruled through secretaries, demonstrating again the monarchical reality of power. Tiberius was, however, a morose recluse. The real problems lay elsewhere.

HELLENISTIC GOD–KING OR ROMAN MAGISTRATE?
What often tempted Augustus' heirs was the glamour of the newly conquered Hellenistic monarchies (Alexander the Great's successors) in the eastern Mediterranean. In these empires, it was usual for kings to be hailed as gods while still alive – more agreeable to impatient young princes than waiting until after death. Also, there was no tedious rigmarole of recruiting officials mainly from the ranks of worthy senators and knights. If charming freedmen (ex-slaves), such as Pallas or Narcissus under Claudius, seemed to be the right choice, they could run government departments.

Above: Marcus Aurelius, sacrificing before the Capitoline Temple in Rome. The emperor was also pontifex maximus, *highest priest.*

AD69–79), solidly Roman in his virtues if honest about his dynastic intentions, the constitutional forms were partly revived. But Vespasian passed on power to his sons, first the charming but short-lived Titus, then his second son, Domitian (reigned AD81–96). Domitian soon revealed himself as a paranoid autocrat, who demanded to be addressed as Lord and God. A vast Flavian palace arose on the Palatine, from which he issued orders. Domitian, inevitably, was assassinated.

Under the "Five Good Emperors" (AD96–180) the Principate seemed to have reached some sort of stability with the Senate. Yet the trend towards absolutism continued. Amid the chaos of the 3rd century, the need for effective rule drowned all forms of opposition until the emperor appeared as he really was: a supreme autocrat.

Germanicus, Tiberius' heir, discovered in AD19 that people in the east were still enthusiastic about worshipping a Roman general as a god if he let them. Germanicus did not, but his son Caligula, his head turned by seemingly unlimited prospects of power if not by illness, did, forcing senators to become priests of his own cult. This was unacceptable and Caligula paid for it in AD41. So, too, did Nero, whose paranoia after the senatorial conspiracy of Piso led to a vicious spiral of reprisals and further conspiracies. Nero succumbed in other ways to the lure of Hellenistic god-kingship. His Domus Aureus, or Golden House, built after the great fire of AD64, was a palace of truly imperial size, eating up acres of prime land in central Rome, with a colossal statue of Nero as sun god just outside it.

The palace was half-demolished after his death. In its place symbolically rose the Flavian Amphitheatre, or Colosseum, an amphitheatre for the people, started by Vespasian. Under Vespasian (reigned

Below: Trajan was an immensely popular emperor – with the army, the Senate, people in Rome and in the provinces. This detail from a triumphal arch in Benevento, southern Italy, commemorates his services to commerce.

REPUBLICAN EXTORTION, IMPERIAL PROBITY

The Roman talent for pragmatism was revealed in governing its huge empire. Through a system of trial and error – at the provinces' expense – the Roman Republic found efficient ways of governing its provinces without a large bureaucracy. But by AD300 the empire was being governed on an almost uniform basis by the central government. By then, the skeletal secretariat of the Republic had been replaced by the top-heavy bureaucracy of the Tetrarchy.

Below: The theatre of Pergamum, the kingdom bequeathed to Rome by its last king in 133BC, which became Rome's first province in Asia.

Above: The fortifications of Syracuse, the greatest Greek city in Sicily, date back to 380BC. When Rome finally captured Syracuse in 211BC, it completed its conquest of the island, making it its first true province.

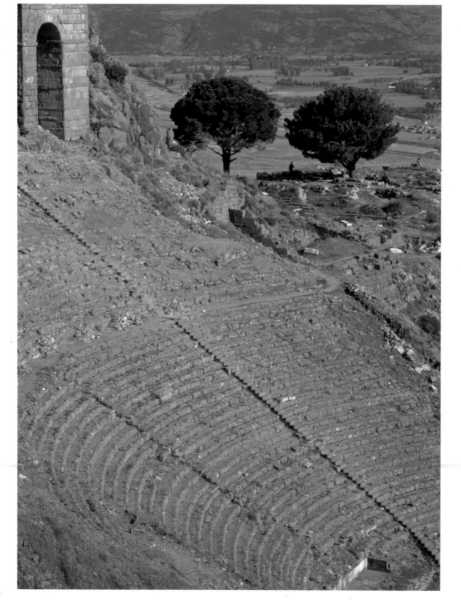

Rome, gaining control of Sicily after the First Punic War in 241BC, faced a new problem. Sicily was large, wealthy and urbanized – mostly by Greek cities but with Punic strongholds in the west, plus rustic Sicel peoples inland. Instead of founding colonies with Roman or Latin rights, as in Italy, Rome created its first *provincia* – literally, sphere of command – appointing former consuls or praetors as governors, with the minimum of staff. Syracuse, the island's largest city, an independent client state until 211BC, offered in its *decuma*, or 10 per cent tax on grain production, a model for revenue-raising. But although many governors corruptly enriched themselves, they also found themselves managing local finances and handing out justice. Sicilian cities, like most cities later in the east, kept much autonomy, being administered by local elected officials later called decurions. These local oligarchs allied with Rome, while Sicily proved an invaluable granary for Rome's hungry citizens. In Spain, too, acquired in 197BC, cities like Cadiz remained client states. A 5 per cent tax on grain output and the development of its silver mines later made Spain into a valuable province, while its tough peoples supplied auxiliary forces. In Italy the Po valley was dominated by warlike Gauls, threateningly close to Rome itself, but offered potentially fine farmland. Another approach led to the founding of such Roman or Latin colonies as Parma and Bologna. By 150BC the Gauls and Ligurians were being driven back into the Alps. By 78BC the area was almost part of Italy in fact if not law; the poet Catullus was born there.

Rome's conquest in the 2nd century BC of the eastern Mediterranean, richer and more civilized than Italy, led to no radical changes in provincial policy. Corrupt governors faced only a small chance of prosecution after their term in office, even if they had flagrantly abused provincials. Cicero's famous lawsuit against Verres, infamous governor of Sicily, was a rare exception. In another speech to the Senate, Cicero pointed out, "Words cannot say how deeply we are hated by foreigners because of the foul behaviour of the men sent out in recent years to govern them." Cicero himself tried to govern Cilicia justly and warned his brother Quintus, on becoming governor of Asia, of the problems caused by well-connected *publicani*, tax-farmers. The burden of Roman taxes, if levied justly, was often no greater than when independent – in the case of Macedonia it was less. But the rapacity of the *publicani* could so enrage provincials – in Greece and Asia Minor in the 80s BC or a century later in Judaea – that they led to anti-Roman uprisings.

PROVINCES UNDER THE EMPIRE
Augustus, who had won the war against Antony as a champion of Italy, could not appear over-generous to provincials. But he still managed to transform provincial administration, usually abolishing the *publicani*. Instead, he levied the *tributum soli*, or land tax. Cisalpine Gaul became part of Italy, and the rest of the provinces

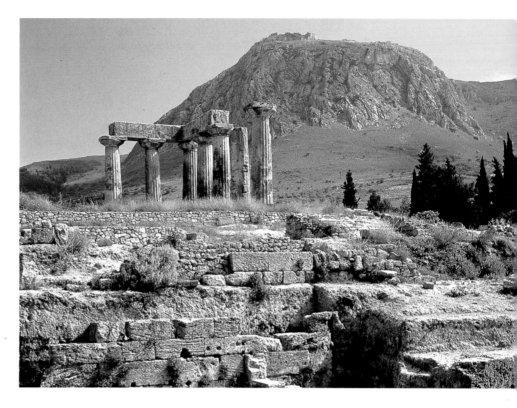

were divided into two groups. Provinces such as Sicily, Africa or Asia were directly under the Senate's jurisdiction, governed by proconsuls, while other regions, such as Gaul and Spain, were part of the *princeps'* giant province, governed by his legates – normally senators, sometimes knights. The founding of cities – whether as colonies of veterans or *civitates*, county towns – made administration easier.

Even in senatorial provinces, good emperors kept a careful eye on governors, as letters between Pliny the Younger, governor of Bithynia, and Trajan show. "Can you send out a land surveyor? A lot of money could be regained…if accurate surveys were made" asked Pliny. Trajan replied, "I regret not. I need all available surveyors here in Rome. Find a reliable one in your own province", and "What is to be done about the unfinished theatre at Nicaea can best be considered and decided by yourself on the spot." But if disaster struck, as when 12 cities in Asia were destroyed in AD17 by an earthquake, even the parsimonious Tiberius promised ten million sesterces in aid and a five-year remission of all taxes, along with a senatorial commission to help in reconstruction.

Above: The temple of Apollo at Corinth, the Greek city sacked by Roman legionaries in 146BC but later reborn as the capital of the province of Achaea. Such a fate was typical of many Greek cities.

Below: These Roman soldiers of the 1st century AD came from Gaul, by then a half-Romanized province.

TAXATION

Above: A cloth merchant displays a piece of fabric, seen on a sarcophagus from Trier in the 4th century AD. The steady growth of textile industries in Gaul and other provinces shows that economic activity was not yet crippled by taxes.

Below: This early 6th-century mosaic from Ravenna was made under Gothic rule. By then, maritime trade had shrunk dramatically, although for centuries maritime taxes had been a major source of revenue for Rome.

"It is a statesman's duty not to impose the *tributum soli* on the people", Cicero declared, voicing the sentiments of the Roman people. The *tributum soli* (property tax) had been the main tax on Roman citizens supposedly levied only in emergencies, and the 3rd century BC had seen one emergency after another. But by the time generals were returning with their booty from a ransacked Greece after the Battle of Pydna, the need for it had passed, and in 167BC it was abolished. Taxes remained controversial throughout the Republic, became less so under the Principate and then, under the later emperors, grew into a crushing burden.

Originally, both Romans and their Latin associates contributed to the Roman state through fighting for it, providing their own arms and armour. Indirect taxes such as customs duties paid for minimal peacetime government, with the *tributum soli* raised in wartime. When the acquisition of Sicily in 241BC allowed the Romans the luxury of taxing subject foreigners, they copied the efficient Syracusan 10 per cent tithe on farm produce. In the wealthier provinces of the east Mediterranean, major problems arose.

PUBLICANI – HATED PROFESSION

In 146BC Achaea (South Greece) and Macedonia were formed into provinces, and 13 years later the last king of Pergamum left his wealthy realm in Asia Minor to Rome. The Republic proved incapable of administering, especially of taxing, these new provinces fairly or honestly. Gaius Gracchus' short-sighted assigning of the tax concessions to the equestrians allowed a ruthless type of tax-collector to emerge: the *publicani*, or tax-farmers (the "publicans" of the New Testament), who could, in effect, levy whatever taxes they liked. The Greek cities supported Mithradates of Pontus in 88BC because of these extortions. Some Romans such as Cicero realized this. Writing to his brother Quintus as the new governor of Asia, Cicero admitted that, "however sympathetic and conscientious you may be in everything, there is one immense obstacle – the *publicani*". After Sulla had driven Mithradates out of Greece in 85BC, he fined the Greek cities five years' back taxes – a sum they could pay only by resorting to Italian money-lenders charging interest at exorbitant rates of 50 per cent or more.

IMPERIAL HONESTY

Julius Caesar and Augustus recognized and tried to remedy this abysmal situation. Augustus could not at first completely abolish the *publicani*, but he regulated them closely. Italy and Rome were exempt from the chief direct tax of the empire, the *tributum soli*, a flat-rate percentage tax on supposed land values, but all parts paid the 1 per cent sales tax, the *centesima rerum venalium*, and customs duties, the *portorium*, levied at 2–2½ per cent and tolls at varying levels in ports. Figures from AD90 from the Red Sea port of Coptos, a terminus for the trade with India, show that a sailor paid tolls of 5 drachmae and a captain 8 – but a prostitute paid 108 drachmae.

A 5 per cent death duty was paid by every Roman citizen, which was one reason why the emperor Caracalla in AD212 granted citizenship to most free people in the empire. Another significant tax was the 5 per cent tax on sales of slaves, again levied throughout the empire. In Egypt, Syria and other parts of the east, Rome also continued to levy the *tributum capitis*, or poll tax, based on censuses that Augustus organized. The emperor Vespasian, restoring the general finances, notoriously put a novel tax on urine collection.

Augustus and his successors had other important sources of income, which supplied the *aerarium militare*, the imperial military treasury. One was from Egypt, long considered separate from the empire, a major source of wheat and other products such as linen and papyrus. Many mines also became imperial possessions, some of the very few large-scale industrial operations in the Roman world. The silver mines near Cartagena in Spain employed 40,000 miners, many of them slaves. The *princeps* had a huge *patrimonium*, or private estate, acquired from legacies or confiscations.

All these together supplied enough, in good times, to pay for the army, the slim civil service and entertaining the Roman populace, without, at first, oppressing the provincials. But it left no surplus for bad times.

THE BURDENSOME LATER EMPIRE
Septimius Severus (AD193–211) raised army numbers to *c*.400,000 men and increased its pay, and under the tetrarchs numbers topped 500,000. There were now four courts to support, and the tax burden increased on a shrinking economy. Ignorant of economics, emperors debased the coinage, hitting the administration worst of all with raging inflation that made soldiers' pay worthless. Gallienus (AD253–68) had to issue a new coinage for his crack troops. Other emperors resorted to the *annona militaris*, military supplies, seizing goods directly.

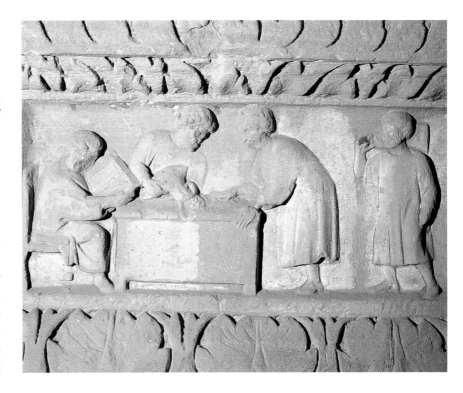

Diocletian undertook a reform of the whole tax system, not completed until after his death. Realizing that the *annona* (the successor to the *tributum*, the tax on land holdings) and the *capitatio*, the poll tax payable in cash, were grotesquely regressive, hitting the poorest hardest, he established a new system: the *capitatio-iugatio*. This was based on the ancient *iugerum*, a plot measuring 60 x 40 yd (55 x 37 m). Land and labour were combined to provide a tax unit that varied according to soil quality and use as vineyard, pasture or cornfield. Five *iugera* of vineyards were worth 20 *iugera* of grain land or 60 of rough pasture. Every five, then every 15, years, a general census, the *indictio*, fixed the tax units, and every year a revised budget and tax demand were issued. Italy lost its tax exemption almost completely. Diocletian aimed to make the burden of taxation not lighter but fairer and more predictable, with some success. Taxes from customs dues and sales continued. He also attempted to stamp out corruption among tax officials and fix maximum prices with an edict in AD301. Under his successors, taxes grew ever heavier until tax collectors were feared and hated more than the barbarians.

Above: A tax-collector from the Rhineland, then under Roman rule, counts his money.

Below: Entrance to the Horrea Epagathiana, a 2nd-century AD warehouse in Ostia. Customs duties at 2½ per cent contributed greatly to imperial revenues.

CHAPTER V

ROME AND THE LAW

The Romans prided themselves on the excellence of their laws, with some reason, seeing law as a field in which they were superior to the Greeks. In its imposing entirety, Roman law is one of Rome's great glories and legacies. However, it did not emerge fully formed, but evolved slowly, from custom and experience, and reached its final form only with the codification of laws by the east Roman emperor Justinian (reigned AD527–65) after the collapse of the empire in the west.

Originally, Roman laws were not at all democratic or concerned with concepts of liberty and justice, but were as pragmatic as the Romans themselves. As early as the 5th century BC, the Romans showed a hard-headed grasp of the day-to-day relations of one citizen to another. For long there was no distinct profession of lawyer and judge, separate from that of law-maker, as today. Cicero was a brilliant barrister, magistrate *and* politician. Under the Principate and later empire, the emperor himself frequently judged cases. Paradoxically, as life in the later empire became increasingly brutal and the imperial administration more despotic, the law became more humane. It was revised and amended by a series of outstanding jurists, influenced by Greek philosophical ideas. Roman law increasingly fused the practical and the idealistic. Its universality, clarity and relative humanity have inspired later jurists and legislators from the Middle Ages to today.

Left: The immense Basilica Nova in Rome became one of the great law courts of the later empire.

LAW IN THE EARLY REPUBLIC
THE TWELVE TABLES OF THE LAW

Above: The altar on this coin, struck at Lyons, the Gallic capital, was for the combined worship of Augustus and Rome itself. The emperor found himself forced to judge more and more law cases, despite the many other demands on his time.

Below: Traditionally, the ten men charged with drawing up the Twelve Tables of the Law in 451BC visited Athens for inspiration, although such a long journey seems improbable for the time.

In the Republic's early decades, there were no written laws. This greatly favoured the patricians, who monopolized the offices of both the *magistrati* and *pontifices*, the priesthood that presided over many law cases, meaning that they alone could interpret laws. *Magistratus* meant both an official and a judge, for the Romans for a very long time made no distinction between judicial law – both criminal and civil – and constitutional laws. *Lex*, a constitutional law, expressed the will of the people (stated by the Assembly, but guided by the Senate), and could be applied to widely differing purposes, such as redistributing land, declaring war or appointing a commander. But a magistrate could also, on his own initiative, issue edicts that had legislative effect. Sitting on a *tribunal* that was literally a platform, the consuls and lesser magistrates were the heirs to the kings, as the emperors were later heirs to the consuls, and heard criminal or civil cases brought before them by plaintiffs. Law,

therefore, in some ways predated actual legislation, being an emanation of Roman *imperium* – authority or power that was thought of as semi-divine in origin.

However, there was nothing mystical about the Twelve Tables. These were drawn up by the decemvirs, a commission of ten patricians who wrote down all Rome's laws on twelve stone tablets in 451BC to placate the plebeians. The laws of the Tables, couched in plain, exact language, remained the basis of Roman law for many centuries, and were learnt by generations of schoolboys. For Livy they were still "the source of entire public and private law". Although possibly influenced by the Greek example of writing down laws, the Twelve Tables' subject matter, as well as their language, is very Roman, a mixture of general principles and minutely detailed private and public law. Among the laws was the *ius provocationis*, the citizen's right to appeal to the Assembly against any magistrate's judgement involving a capital penalty or exile. Later this mutated into "appealing unto Caesar". But this protection was of limited use, as magistrates could still in certain circumstances have a criminal summarily executed without any trial.

Many other laws dealt with the facts of rural life, referring to trees cut down or animals that wandered off – most Romans were still small farmers – but all laws were administered by urban officials. The Twelve Tables generally confirmed the far-reaching paternal power of the father, the *paterfamilias*, over all his children. No matter how mature or important they might be in civil life – even if they had become consuls – sons could not make wills or take part in any legal transaction as long as their fathers were alive. In theory, a father's powers extended to killing his children, although this was

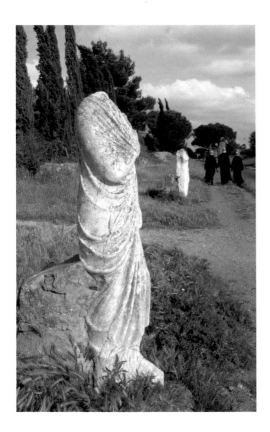

Above: Statues line the great Via Appia to Capua, built by Claudius Appius, who wrote a handbook of legal procedure in 326BC.

rarely exercised. Infanticide (the exposure of children who were unwanted because they were deformed or simply superfluous), on the other hand, was common, especially with baby girls. But women, or at least a *materfamilias*, or wife, did have some rights: for example, on reaching the age of 25 a woman regained the right to manage her own property.

LAW REFORMS

Such stark spelling out of the laws did not help to defuse social tensions, as the decemvirs had hoped, for the plebeians could now see for themselves the iniquities of many existing laws. To redress this, about 30 laws were passed as *leges*, statutes named after their proposer, over the next four centuries, on matters ranging from inheritance to citizenship, sometimes revoking or amending earlier laws considered unjust. A good example of such old laws was that of the *nexus*, in which a debtor who did not repay his

debts risked becoming a *nexus*, or serf – effectively a slave – of his creditors. This law was abolished by the *Lex Poetelia* of 326BC. In 304BC Claudius Appius, a former consul and one of the great radical patricians of Roman history, published a handbook of the correct forms of legal procedure. As the law had until then remained a patrician monopoly, this was another democratizing step.

An even more important decision was made by Titus Corunianus, the *pontifex maximus* in 253BC. The supreme priest (the law was long seen as a manifestation of sacred power) now admitted students to his legal consultations. The priestly monopoly of legal knowledge had already been broken 50 years before by the publishing of judicial procedures, and there was now a need to train others to deal with the expanding number of law cases. These *iurisprudentes*, or lay jurists, were not professional lawyers, but were other citizens, sometimes ex-consuls such as Manius Manilius. Manilius published a book, *Venalium Vendendorum Leges* (Terms of Business for the Sale of Marketable Goods), which attempted to codify and clarify the laws. Attending court cases, the *iurisprudentes* acquired a broad knowledge of the law, which they could use to advise praetors and other magistrates. Their revisions, enlargements and interpretations of the original Twelve Tables, plus their legal formulation of many customary laws that had not been committed to stone, greatly enhanced Roman law. Later they would sit on the *quaestiones*, the special law courts.

Around the same time, in 242BC, a new office of praetor was created, the *praetor peregrinus*, or praetor to deal with legal cases in which at least one of the parties was not a Roman citizen but either a foreigner or subject of Rome. This praetor helped formulate the *ius gentium*, or law of foreign nations, dealing with other nationalities. This was very timely, for Rome had already begun to deal with foreigners who lived not just outside Rome but outside Italy.

Below: One of the strengths of Roman law, from the Twelve Tables of 451BC onwards, was its attention to minute practical detail, which allowed even poorer citizens, such as this woman grocer from Ostia, to practise their trade freely and relatively peacefully.

HOW THE LAWS WORKED IN TIMES OF CRISIS

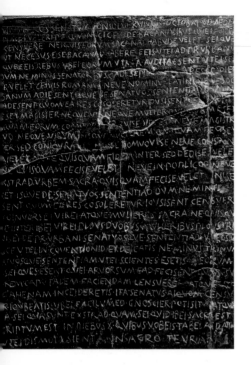

Above: The law De Baccanalis was passed in 186BC to control deteriorating public morality, banning the orgiastic worship of the wine god Bacchus. Later on, the worship of Bacchus, as of many other new foreign gods, was safely regulated.

Right: Marcus Tullius Cicero (106–43BC), orator, writer, statesman and the greatest lawyer of Republican Rome, rose to fame for his attacks on the corrupt governor Verres. His eloquence and rhetoric have given his legal speeches the status of literature.

The events of the century after the start of the Second Punic War in 218BC, when Rome attained Mediterranean predominance and ever-growing wealth for the aristocratic few, saw huge changes in Roman society. The concentration of masses of usually impoverished citizens in Rome – mostly former farmers who had returned from years of fighting abroad to find their land had been occupied by richer neighbours or had gone to waste – led to a dramatic increase in crime, often violent crime. At first, the authorities simply reacted savagely. Hoping to make an example of those they caught, they appointed *tresviri capitales*, triumvirs to deal with capital offences. Such offences included, however, not only the obvious crimes of murder, arson and theft but even the mere carrying of arms with alleged criminal intent or the possession of poisons. If the accused was caught red-handed or confessed his guilt, he would normally be summarily executed. If he pleaded innocence, he would be tried before a praetor or his deputy, or by a triumvir. In both cases, a *consilium*, or advisory commission of jurors, discussed the case and gave advice. In any case, there were no long-term prisons in the Republic and there was a deep repugnance to having armed officers inside the city itself.

As the political situation became more troubled, extraordinary judicial courts (*quaestiones extraordinariae*) were set up to deal with especially egregious cases of corruption, mass crimes, misgovernment and conspiracies against the state. A consul or praetor would preside over these special courts. Finally, from the middle of the 2nd century BC, *quaestiones perpetuae*, or permanent criminal courts, were established to deal with specific offences such as abuse of office by magistrates or conspiracies against the state. The *Lex Sempronia Iudicaria* of 122BC allowed the *equites*, the richer middle class or knights, to sit on the juries, a move made essential because of their rapid growth in number. Although the knights lost control of the courts under Sulla, who restored the Senate's monopoly of them, they were soon reinstated by Pompey and Crassus in 70BC. However, the composition of the juries of the courts remained contentious down to the end of the Republic. Crimes examined by the *quaestiones* included *peculatus*, embezzlement of public funds; *maiestas*, high treason; *de falsis*, forgery of wills and counterfeit coining; *iniuriis*, or violent crimes against the person, and *repetundae*, extortion in the provinces.

THE COURTS

In the courts of the late Republic, which continued under the early Principate, the presiding magistrate would first decide whether a case was worth proceeding with; all prosecutions were still brought by private individuals. He came to his decision after consulting with the members of his *consilium*, the jurors. Jurors for each case were chosen by lot (to avoid corruption or undue influence) to form a panel of up to 75 jurymen, but both prosecution and accused had the right to object to individual jurors, who might be their personal enemies. During the trials the jurors did nothing but listen, leaving the often vituperative courtroom drama to the accused and to the individual prosecutor. Private citizens had either to prosecute and prove their case, or hire somebody else as their advocate, as the Sicilians famously did with Cicero in 70BC. Cicero, who was both a brilliant barrister and a magistrate, a politician and a senator, made Verres lastingly notorious by his speeches against him, accusing him of every kind of crime, from conniving with pirates to stripping the island of so many statues that it damaged the tourist trade. (Verres went into exile rather than face conviction.) Few cases were as colourful as his, however.

In fact, the procedures actually gave some advantages to the accused. Not only was he entitled to several advocates, but he was allowed 50 per cent more time to speak than the prosecution. The jury finally voted in secret on the accused's alleged guilt or innocence. If found guilty, the penalty fixed by the law was ordered by the magistrate. If it were only a matter of a fine, the jurors might meet again to decide the exact amount. Death was the supposed penalty for many offences, but in practice only slaves and people of the lower orders were normally executed. Generally, other citizens were permitted to escape into exile. As life in Rome was widely believed to be the only life worth living, exile seemed punishment enough.

The jury system of the *quaestiones* normally ensured a reasonably fair and balanced dealing with most criminal cases. But these criminal cases were often time-consuming and laborious and could drag on for years and years. Under the Principate, therefore, the *cognitio extra ordinem* of the imperial law court grew in importance. This was an extraordinary criminal procedure without a jury. By the 2nd century AD, jury courts had begun to fade away. Augustus, at first unwilling to involve himself in judicial affairs, increasingly found himself called

on to give judgement in courts, something that a legalistic-minded emperor like Claudius later positively welcomed. In reality, of course, the *princeps* could judge any case, for even in imperial times there were no professional judges; the supreme civil official was also the supreme judge (*iudex*). Through his tribunician power, the *princeps* could also have laws passed, and his decrees were anyway treated as law. The emperor's concern with law continued, indeed intensified, under the later emperors, culminating at last in the emperor Justinian's great code.

Above: A lictor, or ceremonial official, who preceded consuls, is shown carrying the fasces. *This was a bundle of rods with an axe head at one end, symbolizing the powers of capital and corporal punishment that such magistrates wielded.*

THE GREAT IMPERIAL CODIFICATIONS

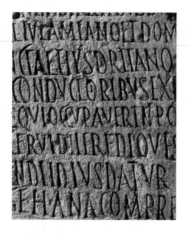

Above: Roman law was not automatically enforced on the provinces. But its superior appeal as the law of Rome meant, as these inscriptions of AD209 from Africa show, that most provinces soon adopted it.

Below: Roman public buildings included great basilicas, where judgements were heard. Their form and plan was adopted by early Christian builders, as at this basilica on the Via Nomentana, Rome.

As the empire grew and more and more subjects became full citizens and fully subject to Roman law, legislation inevitably became more complicated. The need to harmonize accumulated laws variously derived from the Twelve Tables, from magistrates' and emperors' edicts and from the numerous *leges* (statutory laws) became pressing.

THE FIRST CODIFICATIONS

As early as the 1st century BC, Mucius Scaevola, consul in 95BC, produced a handbook on civil law that was long regarded as the standard work. But it was not until the 2nd century AD, under the great organizing emperor Hadrian, that determined attempts were made to codify the law. Hadrian initiated a series of codifications that continued into the 6th century AD.

Iuventius Celsus, who had been consul for the second time in AD129 under Hadrian, wrote 39 books of *digesta*

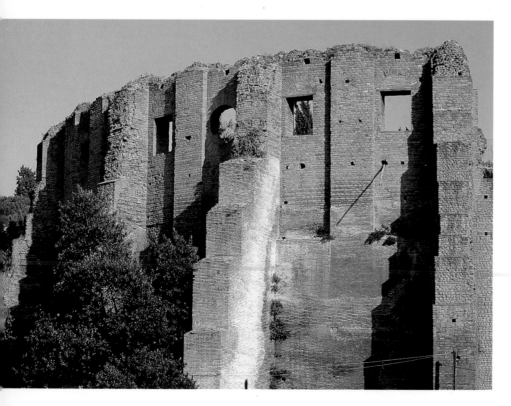

(classified legal decisions). In them, he pronounced numerous celebrated legal definitions and pithy maxims, such as the famous formula *impossibilium nulla obligatio* (*Digesta*, 50), "there can be no legal requirement to do the impossible". Salvius Julianus, who became consul in AD149, collected and revised the edicts that successive praetors had declared during their year in office in his *Edictum Perpetuum*, or everlasting edict, which was the first real codification of Roman law. From that time on, imperial edicts could be recognized as permanently valid legally. His publication helped spread a wider understanding of the legal safeguards protecting the inhabitants of the empire and also revealed a growing humanitarian concern for the empire's subjects – at least on paper.

Slaves now had more legal protection, which circumscribed their owners' rights to treat them completely as chattels. This was partly because they were becoming scarcer and therefore more valuable, but it also marked a change in attitudes. Although both pagan and Christian thinkers abhorred slavery, their views did not reflect a general revulsion, and on economic grounds slavery appeared indispensable. One of Salvius' pupils, Gaius, continued Salvius' work in his *Institutes*, while under Marcus Aurelius (reigned AD161–80), Cervidius Scaevola continued the task of interpreting and codifying the corpus of Roman law. The new basilicas, such as that of Maxentius in Rome, now served as courts where the emperor gave judgement.

Despite the growing political and military troubles of the 3rd century AD, the work of codifying and moderating the laws was carried further. Aemilianus Papinianus, the prefect of the Praetorian guard for ten years (AD203–213) under the militaristic Severans, became famed for his great compendia of the legal decisions that comprised the laws, the *quaestiones* and *responsa* (investigations and findings). Under the emperor Alexander Severus, Domitius Ulpian was a noted lawyer and writer, and adviser to Julia Mammaea. As the emperor's mother was effectively the regent, Ulpian also became Praetorian prefect. His huge works, which endeavoured to cover the full gamut of the laws, are extremely clear and reveal his easy and lucid mastery of very complicated material.

Other distinguished lawyers of the age were Herennius Modestinus, who was prefect of the Vigiles (watchmen) from AD226 to AD244, and Paulus, whose copious writings include the *Sententia* (opinions). Many of these writers either came from the eastern, Greek part of the empire or were deeply influenced by Greek philosophical concepts. Their philanthropic and, in some ways, democratic beliefs modified ancient Roman concerns which had centred on private property and the sanctity of contracts. Paradoxically, just as these high-minded men were writing, the empire was collapsing into a bloody chaos that made all such idealism seem useless.

THE IMPERIAL DIGESTS

Although the empire in the west finally collapsed in the 5th century AD, urban life continued unchecked in the richer and more civilized east. Here, the school of Beirut (in the Lebanon) had emerged as the leading centre of Roman law studies – mostly in Latin – and provided the lawyers who helped draw up the two final grand digests of Roman law. Building on the achievements of Ulpian and other jurists, this led to the Theodosian Code of AD438, issued under the eastern emperor Theodosius II. Accepted in both parts of the empire, this combined humane and enlightened ideals with savagely repressive measures, repeating ineffective laws passed many times before. The majesty of the law was no longer so respected by people in real life.

In the 6th century AD, the eastern empire enjoyed what seemed a golden age under Justinian I (reigned AD527–65). He reconquered half the western empire and enriched Byzantium with numerous palaces and churches, most notably the cathedral of Hagia Sophia. But perhaps his greatest achievement was his enduring *Digest of Roman Law*. Justinian appointed a committee of 16 lawyers to summarize and amalgamate the whole of Roman law. Over 11 years, from AD528, the lawyers compressed three million lines of older laws into a mere 150,000 lines. This gave the Byzantine world its laws for the next millennium, and profoundly influenced law in the then barbarous west. When medieval western Europe rebuilt itself as a civilization, its rulers looked to this great compilation. The jurists who emerged from Europe's oldest university – the University of Bologna – from 1100 onwards, revived and expanded this *Codex* of Roman law. Although it tended to elevate governmental efficiency above individual rights, its comprehensive clarity proved very attractive to successive states, some of them democratic. Under the Napoleonic empire (1803–14), it became the law of almost all continental Europe and, later, of many parts of Latin America.

Above: The Emperor Napoleon's famous legal Code was consciously modelled on Roman law. It forms the basis of much continental European law to this day.

Below: The eastern emperor Justinian I reconquered half the west and built many fine churches, but his greatest achievement was his final codification of Roman law.

POLICE AND SECRET POLICE

Above: The increasingly suspicious emperor Tiberius centralized the crack Praetorian guard in a special camp in Rome, where they were controlled by Sejanus, who was for a long time the emperor's most trusted confidant and minister.

For a long time, the Romans lacked two aspects of civil life that seem essential to modern eyes: a professional local or national police force, with some form of central criminal detective agency, and, perhaps even more notably, a prison service to incarcerate criminals for long-term punishment.

KEEPING ORDER

Under the Republic, from 367BC, policing the (still quite small) city was a task for the four aediles – two plebeian, two patrician – who were elected each year and who maintained public order. Later, the *praetor urbanus* helped deal with the growth in crime. This patchy attempt to deal with crime was common, not just in the ancient world, but right up to the 19th century. (Britain had no proper police force until well into the 19th century and used to

deport those criminals it did not execute, as did the Russians.) In Rome, under the generally light government of the early Principate, minimalist policing worked reasonably well at first, with troops from the Praetorian guard always available as a back-up force. From the time of the Severans (AD193–233), however, secret police, who had already appeared under tyrannical rulers such as Domitian and Commodus, multiplied. The later empire effectively became a police state, whose horrors were limited only by its corruption and incompetence.

In the city of Rome itself, whose population must have passed the million mark in the 1st century AD, some sort of police force was clearly necessary, as Augustus realized. Due to the almost total lack of street lighting – Antioch was the one large city in the empire that had some sort of crude street lights – Rome became a dangerous place at dusk, although the rich went out with their own bodyguards, not over-concerned about what happened to lesser citizens. Augustus created two new forms of police; the *cohortes urbanae* and the *vigiles*. The *cohortes urbanae*, or city cohorts, who comprised first three, then four, cohorts of 500 men, were commanded by a senator, the prefect of the city. The only armed force left directly under the Senate's control, it kept order of a sort in public places. More effective at night were the *vigiles*, or night watchmen/firemen, seven brigades of 1,000 men (one for each two of the city's 14 wards), initially recruited from freedmen, who patrolled the streets at night. They seem, however, to have been more concerned with fighting fire than crime, for they carried buckets and pumps with them, but on their regular patrols through the city they must have also acted as some sort of deterrent to crime. But, despite this, we can assume that Rome remained dangerous at night.

Right: Although theoretically part of the regular army, the Praetorians were in reality treated quite differently. Paid more and retiring earlier, they lived in Rome and often, like this guard, were not obliged to wear full armour.

Backing up these unimpressive forces were the formidable cohorts of the Praetorians, the special guard recruited only from Roman citizens of Italy until the reign of Septimius Severus (AD193–211), paid twice the usual rate and under the command of the Praetorian prefect, the highest post an equestrian could hope to reach. Augustus stationed its nine cohorts around Italy, but under Tiberius they were centralized by Sejanus into a large camp in the north-east of Rome. These were the imperial guard, however, not used for day-to-day policing but to suppress popular riots or conspiracies. Although the *Pax Romana* established by Augustus meant an end to large-scale brigandage, there were still plenty of robbers around, even in the mountains of Italy, and at times small-scale military operations were needed to suppress them. Elsewhere in the empire, the army was occasionally called in to deal with major uprisings: from the Sicilian slave revolts of 135BC, when 70,000 slaves united under their "king" Antiochus to defy the Romans for three years, to the revolt of the Bagaudae (literally, brigands) who, from the 3rd century AD on, terrorized central Gaul, setting up their own courts. In between such uprisings, decurions, the local magistrates of the cities around the empire, dealt adequately with local crime on a smaller scale, acting as judges.

THE POLICE STATE

Like all military dictatorships, the emperors made use of *delatores*, spies or informers, who discovered or invented conspiracies, and *speculatores*, special mounted intelligence officers of the Praetorian guard – regular officials, unlike the *delatores* – who sometimes travelled around the empire. But the wiser emperors did not rely too much on such doubtful sources. Despite this, Trajan – *optimus princeps*, or the best of emperors, in the Senate's view – started a new form of intelligence service, the *frumentarii*. This grew rapidly under Septimius

Severus, augmented by similar officials, who set up the sinister office of the *agentes in rebus*, literally those active in public affairs; the *stationarii*, or place-holders, and *collectiones*, or tax-collectors. These special police were usually soldiers, indicating the militarization of society under the Severans. According to the early 20th-century historian M.I. Rostovtzeff, they did not "care a straw for the people", but hunted down those who had defaulted on their taxes or gone into hiding to escape government extortions.

Diocletian's bureaucratic reforms encouraged a huge growth in the number of these officials. Later, in the 360s, the emperor Julian introduced measures to try to reduce their numbers. Such agents were solely concerned with protecting the government and lining their own pockets, not with dealing with normal crime or helping the people, whose well-being and safety held no interest for them. Bribery was the normal means by which most subjects of the later empire dealt with such imperial officials.

Above: Trajan created a new form of intelligence officer, the frumentarii, *who thrived under later, less benign emperors.*

Below: The arch of Septimius Severus, the militaristic emperor in whose reign the secret police multiplied.

PUNISHMENT

Above: This mosaic of the 3rd century AD shows gladiators battling. Due to the inevitably high mortality rate of this, perhaps the most brutal spectator sport ever devised, many criminals were condemned to be gladiators.

Below: The Romans' formidable organizing powers are exposed in the underground network of passages that kept the Colosseum in Rome working smoothly in the long games that filled so many days.

Two things characterize Roman attitudes to punishment. First, there was no real equality before the law, which we tend to take for granted. Second, keeping criminals imprisoned for long periods was impractical, on grounds of expense, and other penalties were the norm.

BREAKING THE LAW

There was a marked division between the way Roman citizens and non-citizens were treated, both under the Republic and under the early Principate. Later, after almost everybody had become a citizen in AD212, an even starker division grew up between the treatment of the upper classes, *honestiores*, and the lower, *inferiores*. Even in the Republic, richer citizens such as senators and knights were better treated than poorer ones.

Roman jails were normally manned by soldiers, and used only in the short term as a place for suspects awaiting trial. Punishments were often gruesome, especially for non-Roman citizens or *inferiores*. In civilian life, Roman citizens, and later the *honestiores*, could not be flogged or crucified, for example, and could "appeal to Caesar", as St Paul did when kept on remand. And while it was widely believed that slaves would tell the truth only if they were severely tortured, citizens were exempt from torture.

Early Rome was essentially a primitive rustic society, and most penalties in the early and middle Republic were draconian, with crude punishments that seem violent to our modern sensibilities. In Rome's deeply conservative culture, such punishments long remained on the books. For example, Vestal Virgins were chosen from high-born Roman maidens around the age of 7 to tend the fire of Vesta, the goddess of the hearth. The girls had to remain virgins for their 30 years of service, by which time they were regarded as being well past marriage. Inevitably, some lapsed and had sexual liaisons. If they were discovered, they faced the potential sentence of being buried alive. Much later, Domitian's revival of this archaic punishment shocked the then more tolerant Romans. Parricide also incurred punishments that reveal the deep religious revulsion that it aroused. The offender was tied up and bundled into a sack with a snake and a cock and then hurled off a rock.

Many penalties, of course, related to civil laws. An article from the Eighth Table of the Law, concerned with penalties, states, "If any man mutilates another's limbs, he must suffer the same, unless he agrees to pay compensation to the injured man." This *Lex Talionis*, the law of an eye for an eye, extended to other crimes, such as arson: arsonists themselves should be burnt alive. The Tables even stipulated the death penalty for any patron – who was almost always a nobleman – who cheated his client, though this was not often enforced. In all these types of cases, it was not the Roman state but individual citizens who brought the actions, the state merely supervising their private pursuit of justice.

EXILE

Although death was a penalty for many offences, it was not always enforced, especially for more important Roman citizens. Instead, exile remained a common and potent penalty. Not only did it end a Roman's political life – for the time being, anyway – but it meant banishment from the one city on earth that really mattered to all true Romans. The incorrigibly metropolitan poet Ovid was exiled to the barbarous remoteness of Tomis on the Black Sea by Augustus in AD8, possibly for involvement in the affairs that led also to the banishment of Augustus' own daughter Julia.

LIONS AND GLADIATORS

Although the image of Christian martyrs being thrown to the lions – tied to a stake in the arena and there chewed to death – remains powerful, Christians in fact made up only a few of the people who were sentenced to this *damnatio ad bestias*, or condemnation to the wild beasts. This form of punishment was anyway not thought particularly entertaining by Romans, the most exacting of audiences.

Many criminals condemned to death ended up in the arena as gladiators, people utterly without rights. From the 2nd century BC on, Rome was developing an insatiable appetite for gladiators, who had a high mortality rate. The games Titus gave for the inauguration of the Colosseum in AD80 required several thousand pairs, some of whom were killed during the day's entertainment. But gladiators were very expensive to train, and combat did not inevitably end in death. Those who survived three years in the games were normally given their wooden sword of freedom.

Special schools of gladiators, with ferocious discipline, were established. One of the most famous of these was at Capua, and it was here that the last great slave revolt broke out in 73BC, organized by the Thracian gladiator Spartacus. Displaying genuine leadership, he united his fellow outcasts and for two years

kept the forces of Rome at bay, moving around the mountains of southern Italy until Crassus cornered and killed him in 71BC in Apulia. Along the great Via Appia from Capua to Rome, 7,000 ex-gladiators were then crucified as a ghastly warning to other potential rebels.

CRUCIFIXION

The last, worst and most degrading punishment of Rome's sadistic society was crucifixion. An excruciatingly slow torture (for few had their deaths hastened by a spear like Jesus Christ), crucifixion was adopted by the Romans in the 2nd century BC, probably from the Asian monarchies. Julius Caesar had the pirates who captured him crucified, the normal punishment for such heinous crimes as well as for conspiracy. After the conversion of Constantine and his successors to Christianity in the 4th century AD, crucifixion was discontinued, but this was on religious rather than humanitarian grounds.

Above: Special training schools for gladiators were established in the late Republic to satisfy the insatiable demand of the Roman populace for such brutal thrills.

Below: Crucifixion was a common, if horrifically painful, form of death penalty. It was used for many crimes, from piracy to conspiracy.

CHAPTER VI

FOREIGN POLICY

Although Rome had no foreign office or state department, it certainly had policies towards the non-Roman world. While well-meaning Romans such as Cicero liked to believe that Rome acquired its empire chiefly in wars of self-defence, others must have seen it differently, as they watched the smoke rising from Carthage, Syracuse, Corinth – all cities sacked by Rome.

Yet for a long time Rome, unlike the Persians or the Macedonians under Alexander, initiated few wars of deliberate conquest. From *c.*300BC to Pompey's eastern command in 66BC, Rome's foreign policy was more reactive than pre-emptive. Only when control of foreign policy slipped from the Senate's grasp did clear signs of expansionist imperialism appear, first under Pompey and then under Caesar and his successors. After that, Rome followed an aggressively expansionist policy until it could do so no longer and was forced to go on the defensive in the 2nd century AD.

All other cities had to be subordinated to Rome and were regarded as foreign, even when they were Latin-speaking neighbours. However, the privileges of Roman citizenship were gradually extended to inhabitants of other city-states, first in Italy, then across the Mediterranean world. Ultimately, after the conquest of Egypt in 30BC, there were no foreign powers worthy of the name, except for the Parthians in the east. Instead, there was the Roman world – and the barbarians.

Left: A sculpted head from the ruins of Carthage, the North African city that was for long Rome's deadliest enemy.

EARLY BEGINNINGS
THE CONQUEST OF ITALY

Above: The Via Appia, the first and archetypal Roman road, was designed for the conquest of southern Italy as much as for communication.

Below: This fresco from a 4th-century BC tomb near Paestum, southern Italy, shows warriors armed like the Samnites. The Samnites were Rome's most threatening enemies in the region, taking three wars to subdue.

Although it may sound grandiloquent to talk of the foreign policy of a state whose territory in 500BC was roughly only 10 miles (16km) across, Rome regarded all those beyond its sacred *pomerium*, or city boundary, as foreign. By binding such cities to her in treaties, at times granting them citizenship or alliance, Rome's approach became less "divide and rule" than "conquer and assimilate". Even large, relatively distant cities such as Capua could be incorporated by this incremental method, Rome's most original idea in conquering Italy.

Rome signed a treaty with the cities of the Latin League in 493BC, but she did so only because mountain enemies were threatening farms in the lowlands. These tribes were only ejected from the key Algidus Pass in about 430BC, after a 50-year war. They were overcome by establishing chains of *coloniae* – defensive settlements of farmer–soldiers who received land. At first these were federal Latin colonies, with Romans merely among other settlers, but later Rome began founding her own colonies, which then became civilian settlements too.

Another way of dealing with enemies was assimilation. The Sabines were other menacing neighbours in the hills north-east of Rome, but around 505BC the Sabine nobleman Attus Clausus settled by invitation in Rome, reputedly taking 4,000 followers with him and increasing the city's population. He became a Roman patrician and changed his name to Claudius, founder of the Claudians. Afterwards, the Romans imported the Sabine god Sancus, which symbolized the fusion of the two peoples.

A less malleable threat was Veii. Just 11 miles (18km) north of Rome, this wealthy Etruscan city controlled a network of paved roads and blocked Rome's way north. Wars started in 479BC, until finally the Romans began such a long siege – traditionally, ten years from 406–396BC – that the army had to be paid for the first time. Veii was destroyed, its people killed or enslaved and its patron goddess Juno taken to Rome, thereby symbolizing triumph in a total war. This extermination of a city – along with taking its land for the *ager publicus*, public land – was often repeated.

All such successes seemed to be overthrown by the invasion of the Gauls in *c*.390BC, who sacked the still unwalled city. In despair, some citizens even talked of abandoning their burnt city for Veii until Camillus rallied them. The small city of Caere helped Rome recover and in return received *hospitium publicum*, reciprocal rights with Roman citizens in judicial and financial matters. Rome later extended this formula to other cities. In 378BC Rome fortified itself with the

Samnite League 298 BC
Roman territory 298 BC
Carthaginian possessions *c.* 260 BC
Roman colonies by 272 BC
Under Roman control 270 BC
Annexed by Rome 263 BC

Left: By 265BC Rome controlled the whole of peninsular Italy south of a line from Pisa to Rimini. Besides territories directly part of the Republic and full Roman colonies – strategically planted from Rimini in the north to Brindisi in the south and often linked by roads – there were allied territories, enjoying either Latin or the less prestigious Italian status. All these cities proved a source of vital strength in Rome's forthcoming contest with Carthage, but important long-established Greek cities such as Tarento were sometimes disloyal.

Below: The Etruscans were Rome's most impressive and powerful neighbours. They were wealthy, civilized and had a high level of culture as shown in this life-size terracotta sculpture of a married couple from a 6th-century BC Etruscan tomb.

Servian walls, but it was already expanding again. In 381BC Tusculum, a Latin League city, received full Roman citizenship to keep it loyal to Rome. This novel generosity was later extended to other cities, also usefully boosting the numbers of citizens for military service.

In 343BC Capua, the wealthiest city of fertile Campania, appealed to Rome for help against Samnite raiders. Initially, the war went badly. Roman troops mutinied at having to fight so far from home, and the Latin League, alarmed at Rome's power, joined the Volscians against her. Four years of bitter fighting were required to defeat the Latins by 338BC. Then Rome dissolved the League, treating each city differently. The citizens of Lanuvium, for example, received full Roman rights, as did three other deserving Latin cities. The Volscian city of Antium on the coast, a pirate stronghold, had its ships destroyed – their beaks went to adorn the *Rostra* in Rome – and a Roman colony was planted, which the Volscians were allowed to join. Capua and four other Campanian cities then received Roman citizenship *sine suffragio*, without the vote. The Romans showed themselves fair and pragmatic in these treaties, winning the abiding loyalty of most cities.

OVERLORD BY DEFAULT

Above: Two Greek hoplites (heavy infantrymen) from an Attic vase. Adaptable Roman legionaries repeatedly defeated Greek hoplites massed in the inflexible phalanx, *a major reason for Rome's final total success in the eastern Mediterranean region.*

Below: The Colossus of Rhodes, a giant statue reputedly straddling the harbour entrance, symbolized Rhodes' maritime wealth and power. When its power was wrecked by Rome's expansion, piracy flourished, no longer checked by the Rhodian navy.

There seemed little reason for a major conflict between the Roman Republic, a land power controlling peninsular Italy, and Carthage, a mercantile power based in modern Tunisia, with trade routes extending to southern Spain. Treaties going back to the first days of the Roman Republic were renewed as late as 279BC. But when Rome faced Sicily across the Straits of Messina, it faced new dilemmas. An appeal to Rome by a party in Messina for help against Carthage left the Senate undecided until the Assembly, exercizing its right to declare war, decided for action. The bloody wars made Rome hegemon (ruler) of the Mediterranean.

One reason for supporting Messina was that the Greeks of southern Italy wanted Roman help for Greeks in Sicily, but this counted for little compared with a new aggressive mood in Rome itself. Carthage, too, had been trying to extend its control over all Sicily from its base at Palermo in the west and was determined to control the Straits of Messina. About three times larger than Rome, an immensely wealthy city, with a huge professional fleet and mercenary armies, Carthage was Rome's one significant rival power in the western Mediterranean. As such, Rome was unlikely to ignore it indefinitely.

Victorious after the First Punic War in 242BC, Rome's policy towards Carthage was mixed. Rome helped Carthage suppress a massive revolt by unpaid mercenaries in 239BC, for social order had to be maintained. But it then took advantage of Carthaginian preoccupation to annex Sardinia and Corsica, both in the Carthaginian sphere, in an act of aggression. Marseilles, a Greek city allied to Rome, was worried about growing Carthaginian power in Spain that threatened Ampurias, its colony in Catalonia. (Possibly Hamilcar Barca signed a treaty in 227BC accepting the river Ebro as his northern frontier in Spain.) When Hannibal attacked Saguntum in 219BC, independent if south of the Ebro, Rome decided on war – superfluously, as it turned out, as it was Hannibal who launched the catastrophic Second Punic War.

The final act, the Third Punic War of 146BC, showed Rome at it most odious. Carthage had regained its wealth through agriculture and trade but, lacking a large fleet, posed no threat. However, the Romans, even without reminders from Cato the Censor that *Carthago delenda est* (Carthage must be deleted), had grown greedy. They destroyed Carthage after a long siege, enslaving its citizens. By then, Rome was mistress of the middle sea.

ARBITER OF THE EAST

The eastern Mediterranean around 200BC was dominated by three great Hellenistic kingdoms ruled by descendants of Alexander's generals: the Ptolemies in Egypt, the Antigonids in Macedonia and the Seleucids, whose huge Asian empire centred on Syria. Smaller Hellenistic states included Rhodes, a cultured trading republic, the Aeotolian

Above: Hoplites formation from a Greek amphora from Chigi, Italy. By adopting new tactics, Rome defeated such Greek armies.

Confederacy in Greece and the Attalid kingdom of Pergamum in Asia Minor. For a century these states had been involved in complex alliances and wars that seldom caused serious damage. Upon entering this civilized sphere, Rome proceeded to wreck it through myopic fear, suspicion and greed that together made it look more imperialist than it really was.

Philip V of Macedonia had rashly allied himself with Hannibal in 215BC, angering Rome, although the First Macedonian War involved little fighting. When Philip made a secret treaty with Antiochus III of Syria in 202BC to divide Ptolemaic lands, Rome intervened. Flaminius defeated Philip at Cynoscephalae in 197BC, where Roman legions out-manoeuvred the Macedonian *phalanx*, but he merely reduced Macedonia's size. To the cities of Greece proper, Flaminius promised liberty. This promise was genuine, except that he envisaged a sort of patronage, not the total independence the delighted Greeks assumed. From this misunderstanding came much grief. Meanwhile Antiochus, until then a successful ruler, made a series of clumsy mistakes: he seized the Gallipoli peninsula, although Rome had told him to keep out of Europe; he welcomed Rome's arch-enemy Hannibal to his court in 195BC; and sent a force into Greece in 192BC to support the rebellious Aetolians. Rome, alarmed that

he wanted to recreate Alexander's empire, sent armies to defeat Antiochus at Thermopylae and again, massively, at Magnesia in 190BC. Antiochus lost all land west of the Taurus Mountains and paid a huge indemnity. Rome was now arbiter of the east, a point ruthlessly brought home to the next Seleucid, Antiochus IV, when he invaded Egypt in 168BC. The Roman envoy Popilius Laenas drew a circle around the king and told him not to move until he agreed to Rome's terms. Antiochus humbly accepted.

Rome did not fill its hegemonic role well. Many Romans enriched themselves in Greece, while Rome still declined to govern Greece. When the Achaean League rebelled in 146BC, Rome sacked Corinth, Greece's richest city, enslaving its citizens and creating a province. Rome treated its allies scarcely better. Fearing the growing power of Rhodes, it created a free port at Delos that wrecked Rhodes' maritime wealth. With Rhodes in decline, piracy flourished unchecked, also hurting Rome. Attalus III, last king of Pergamum, accepting the inevitable, bequeathed his kingdom to *imperium populi Romani*, the empire of the Roman people, in 133BC.

Below: The Acropolis of Pergamum, the capital of the wealthy Eumenid kingdom in west Asia Minor. Pergamum was long Rome's chief ally in the east, its cavalry helping to defeat the Seleucids at the Battle of Magnesia in 190BC.

DEFENSIBLE FRONTIERS
THE RHINE AND THE DANUBE

Above: Pompey, one of the Republic's finest generals, added a whole string of provinces and client states to Rome's eastern empire.

Below: A bend of the River Rhine in Germany. Fast-flowing, the Rhine offered a natural but not inevitable frontier for the empire in northern Europe. It effectively marked Rome's north-western boundary for almost 450 years.

The intermittent expansion of the empire in the middle Republic gave way to rapid, even reckless expansion in the 1st century BC. Between 66 and 63BC, Pompey extended the Roman sphere of influence from the Caucasus to the Red Sea. Caesar conquered the huge area of *Gallia Comata* ("long-haired Gaul") a decade later, and claimed Britain as a client state. Augustus annexed Egypt, the richest kingdom of the Mediterranean, in 30BC. His later wars of conquest added north-west Spain to the empire by 23BC, the Alpine lands by 15BC and most of the Balkans and Danubian territories by 6BC. Later, Tiberius and Drusus conquered as far as the Elbe by AD5, while Roman fleets even nosed into the Baltic. Roman power seemed set on an endless advance. The question was, where would the *termini imperii*, the frontiers of the empire, finally be set, if the empire were not to continue to advance north-east indefinitely? Fixed frontiers, a new concept for Rome, required choosing defensible lines, tactically and strategically.

There was no compelling reason to regard the Rhine or the Danube as definitive frontiers. Despite Caesar's claims in his *De Bello Gallico* about the importance of the Rhine, neither of these two great rivers marked a real cultural or political divide. Augustus, while happy to ignore Britain beyond the seas, decided to conquer Germany between the Rhine and the Elbe, presumably to create a line running roughly from Hamburg through Dresden and Prague to Vienna (none of these cities existed then, of course). This would usefully shorten the frontier, as later emperors realized. Accordingly, a pincer campaign was launched in AD6. Tiberius was to advance north through Bohemia, while other troops moved up the Elbe and others up the Main valley past what is now Frankfurt. But a massive revolt in recently conquered Pannonia recalled Tiberius for three years' bitter campaigning, the worst, according to Tacitus, since the Punic Wars. Then Varus (an army commander) and his three legions were betrayed and massacred by Arminius of the Cherusci in the Teutoburg Forest in AD9. Augustus, now an old man, was shattered by the news and called a halt to all further expansion.

Tiberius followed Augustus' advice to stay within the bounds of the empire to the letter, keeping the Rhine–Danube lines, but this was not very practical. Although both rivers were large, the L-shaped re-entrant angle between their upper reaches was vulnerable to invasion. Claudius, eager for military glory, invaded Britain in AD43, embroiling Rome in a province with a frontier problem in its north that was not settled until Hadrian's visit in AD122. Apart from the suppression of a large-scale revolt by Civilis on the lower Rhine in AD70, Germany was ignored until Vespasian and his sons, especially Domitian, began a new campaign. Systematic and inglorious, this was mocked by Tacitus, but proved of lasting value. In the Chattan War of AD83–5, Domitian pushed the Rhine frontier east, along the line of the Taunus Mountains, creating a fortified frontier that sheltered the Rhineland behind and projected Roman power deeper into Germany. The frontier then ran south along the Neckar to join the upper Danube. Further additions to extend this new area of Agri Decumates to the Danube at Regensburg came in the 2nd century AD, reducing the Rhine–Danube lines by 150 miles (240km) in total; legions could now move far more swiftly from one frontier to another.

DANUBIAN PROBLEMS

Domitian had been distracted from his German campaign by a Dacian attack in AD85. Well organized, rich (thanks to gold mines) and well protected by their mountainous terrain, the Dacians were a growing threat. After Domitian's campaigns produced a stalemate, it was left to Trajan to deal with Dacia. An initial campaign in AD101 with 13 legions (totalling over 150,000 troops) seemed to have made Dacia an obedient client state, but the settlement, weighted in Rome's favour, failed to last. Trajan prepared for another full-scale invasion by building an immense bridge and road. The final storming of the Dacian capital in AD106 meant Dacia became a province, protected along its northern flank by the Limes Porolissensis, a new fortified frontier along the Carpathians. By creating this great bulwark of a province protruding north-east almost on to the Russian steppes, Trajan divided the tribes on either side of it, so safeguarding the Danubian lands for generations. Beyond them, of course, lay Italy itself, almost unprotected.

The Danube frontier collapsed when the Quadi and Marcomanni (from the modern Czech Republic) poured into Italy in AD166. In a series of campaigns, Marcus Aurelius painstakingly drove

them back. Despite being distracted by a rebellion in Syria in AD175, Marcus won a great final victory over the Marcomanni and Quadi in AD179 and was seemingly about to create two new trans-Danubian provinces, Marcomania and Sarmatia, when he died – and with him died his expansionist plans.

Renewed barbarian pressures in the 3rd century AD saw a general retreat on the northern frontier: Aurelian evacuated Dacia by AD275 and the Agri Decumates were abandoned by c.AD265. In their place came new, heavily fortified capitals near the frontiers, such as Trier and Sirmium, with other massive fortresses that barbarians could bypass but never capture. The whole empire had in some ways become the front line.

Above: Roman troops on the Danube embarking supplies. The Danube became Rome's longest, and ultimately most vulnerable, frontier.

DEFENSIBLE FRONTIERS
ASIA

The best advice for western generals is, "Never invade Russia." For Romans, the advice should have been, "Don't invade Parthia", for it proved fatal to many military reputations. Parthia's huge empire, which stretched from the Syrian frontier to central Asia, was unimpressive militarily. Its kings faced revolts from over-mighty subjects in its Iranian lands, while the Hellenistic cities of Mesopotamia (Iraq) felt little loyalty to it. Its large armies were not professional like the Romans', although their cavalry was well suited to the terrain. Such weakness allowed Rome to invade Parthia at times, but geography – the huge distances, the deserts, the way

the Iranian highlands outflanked the Tigris–Euphrates valley – in the end prevented it ever from holding more than north Mesopotamia. Unfortunately, the precedent of Alexander the Great, who had conquered half of Asia, lured Roman generals east. When the formidable Sassanian dynasty replaced the Parthians in the AD220s, Rome faced worse problems. What had been a quiet frontier became a perilous burden. Yet the frontier between the upper Euphrates and the Tigris fluctuated remarkably little for six centuries.

Rome and Parthia first clashed after Pompey annexed the Syrian rump of the Seleucid empire in 64BC. Crassus, who was

Above: Petra was a wealthy trading city (now in Jordan), and it was annexed under the emperor Trajan.

Right: The Eastern frontier c.AD300. Palmyra's short-lived empire (shaded), did not alter the eastern frontier, but Julian's defeat led to the ceding of Nisibis and half of Roman Mesopotamia to Persia.

	Border of Roman Empire c. AD 300
	Kingdom of Palmyra AD 260–272
→	Palmyran invasions
→	Persian raids
→	Julian's invasion of Persia AD 363
✕	Battles

governor of Syria and eager for glory, marched east, to be destroyed with his army by Parthian horse archers in the desert near Carrhae in 53BC. Caesar was preparing an immense invasion of Parthia in 44BC when he was assassinated. Antony, in control of the east after 42BC, decided to attack by the mountain route but failed to capture the key city of Phraapsa in 36BC, when his siege engines were cut off. He had to beat a humiliating retreat harassed by Parthian horsemen. Augustus, after settling other frontiers, was expected to resume the eastward drive but wisely contented himself with a diplomatic triumph in 20BC. This saw the lost legions' eagles (along with a few prisoners) ceremoniously returned and a Roman protégé installed on the Armenian throne. Such client states served as useful buffers between the two powers. For a century, Augustus' successors remained west of the Euphrates, although Vespasian annexed some client states.

BETWEEN TWO RIVERS

There was therefore no need for Trajan's grand eastern venture that began in AD114 with the conquest of Armenia. Mesopotamia may have looked similar to Syria – a fertile land, Aramaic-speaking peasants, Greeks in the cities – and there was talk of securing the trade routes east, but it was Alexander's example that really counted. Failure to take Hatra, right in the middle of the new conquests, signalled that the Parthians were not totally defeated and they began to attack the now long-exposed eastern flanks. Even without the many Jewish revolts behind, these new frontiers were indefensible. Hadrian pulled back completely, apart from Nabatea. The status quo was restored, except that Arabia Nabatea was fortified.

In AD165 the Romans retaliated to the Parthian attack by sacking both Ctesiphon (Baghdad), the Parthian capital, and Hellenistic Seleucia-on-the-Tigris, bringing home a crippling plague and almost wrecking Hellenism in Iraq. But the only significant change was to advance the frontier to Dura-Europus, a fortified city on the Euphrates. This left the rest of the frontier as before, between the upper Tigris and Euphrates, stretching from the Black Sea to the Red, with Palmyra as a client state. But there was one possible line that offered Rome a defensive frontier that Septimius Severus saw and seized. In AD197 he captured Ctesiphon but sagely withdrew, annexing only upper Mesopotamia, following the line of the Khabur river as it flowed south into the Euphrates, then east along the escarpment of the Jebel Sinjar to the Tigris north-east of Nisibis. This territory gave Syria, with its wealthy cities, far more protection and also helped Rome to control Armenia, blocking the Parthians' lowland route to it.

This proved a lastingly defensible frontier. Despite the newly aggressive Sassanid Persian dynasty – it claimed all the old Persian empire's lands up to Macédonia – the Romans retained this new province of (upper) Mesopotamia throughout the 3rd-century crises.

Above: The ruins of Dura-Europus, Syria, a vital fortress on the Euphrates, captured and destroyed after a siege by the Persians in C.AD256 and never reoccupied. The defence of the eastern frontier depended heavily on such fortified trading cities.

CLIENT AND BUFFER STATES

Above: Giant heads c.50BC proclaim the power of the client kings of Commagene.

Below: Pompey entered the Temple in Jerusalem, thereby desecrating it in Jewish eyes.

When Pompey marched through western Asia from the Caucasus to the Red Sea in 66–63BC, annexing and rearranging kingdoms, he recognized many existing smaller kingdoms as client states or allies. The careful use of client or buffer states allied to and to varying degrees under the control of Rome became a characteristic policy of Roman imperialism in the late Republic and early Principate.

Such statelets – most were very small – could supply reinforcements when called for, rather than perpetually requiring costly garrisons themselves. In AD67, Vespasian's legions were reinforced by 15,000 lighter troops from nearby client states for the Jewish war. For Augustus and his heirs, this was an attractive way of defending the empire on the cheap. It resembled the client system in Rome itself and meant, furthermore, that the states concerned often became half-Romanized, or further Hellenized, before being incorporated into the empire. Armenia was the one significant exception to this trend.

Most client kingdoms lined the indeterminate eastern frontier, beyond which loomed the Parthian empire, Rome's only civilized rival. In northern Europe the various German tribes were, for the most part, too fragmentary or impermanent to be able to create stable kingdoms. Here subsidies and treaties kept these barbarians in check or at each others' throats, but they were not proper client kings.

The major eastern client states, established by Pompey and confirmed by Mark Antony and Augustus, included three vital border crossings: Pontus, on the south coast of the Black Sea, Cappadocia in central Asia Minor, annexed in AD17, and Commagene, controlling the vital passage across the upper Euphrates. This latter was ruled by a dynasty of Hellenized monarchs called Antiochus, whose gigantic heads adorn their hilltop mausoleum at Nemrud Dag. Further south, Arab client kings included Palmyra, rising to wealth, and flourishing Arabia Nabatea (Jordan), with its capital at Petra.

Most important and troublesome was Judaea, later Palestina. Herod I the Great ruled from 37 to 4BC, rebuilding the Temple in Jerusalem and building a second coastal capital at Caesarea Maritima, which became a typical Hellenistic city. He was a tyrannical but effective ruler. After his death, his kingdom was divided between his less competent heirs, until its central portion became a Roman province in AD6. (Its most notorious governor was Pontius Pilate.) It returned briefly to Jewish rule under Cornelius Julius Agrippa, Herod's nephew, and his son Cornelius Agrippa II. As their names suggest, these rulers were half-Romanized.

Another client state was Mauretania (northern Algeria/Morocco), formed partly from the old kingdom of Numidia. Its monarch, Juba, became an exemplary Hellenizing king in his new capital at Caesarea and married one of Cleopatra's daughters. It was annexed by Claudius, who also annexed the client state of Thrace in the eastern Balkans. On the north Black Sea, the Bosphoran kingdom was part-Scythian but had Greek cities on the coast. It remained an important client state to Rome because of the grain trade from the Ukraine.

Vespasian annexed Commagene and other smaller client states in a fit of centralizing enthusiasm in AD69–79 until only the tiny kingdoms of the Caucasus – Iberia in the Caucasus, and Colchis – plus Palmyra and Arabia Nabatea remained. This required the deployment of more troops and the building of more forts to face Parthia directly. Trajan annexed Arabia Nabatea in AD106.

ARMENIA: THE EXCEPTION

On the high plateau between Iran and Asia Minor, Armenia formed a natural buffer state between Rome and Parthia (later Persia). Almost independent, it leaned worryingly towards Parthia, being more Iranian than Hellenic with a feudal aristocracy and few towns. Its key position above Syria and Mesopotamia meant that it could not be ignored. Lucullus was the first Roman to enter Armenia, pursuing Mithradates in 69BC. In 65BC Pompey added Armenia to his clients, but Antony's attempt to win it failed. Yet when Augustus staged a triumph in the east in 20BC that returned the legionary standards lost by Crassus at Carrhae, Parthia (temporarily) recognized Armenia as a Roman protectorate. Nero's fine general Corbulo imposed a compromise in AD63 in which Parthian princes would be the kings of Armenia but invested (crowned) by Rome. In AD66 Nero invested Tiridates as king of Armenia in an extravagant ceremony in Rome. Trajan used the Parthian

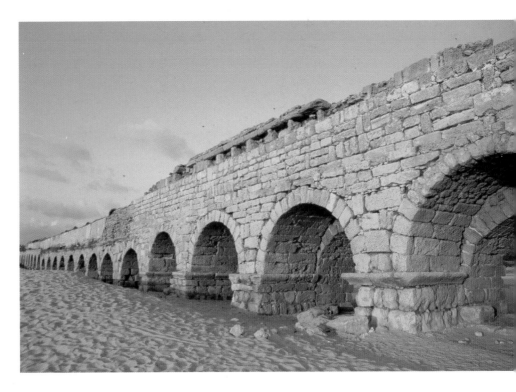

replacement of a Roman-approved king in Armenia in AD114 as a pretext for his grand eastern campaign, annexing the kingdom. Hadrian then evacuated it with other eastern conquests. This seesaw continued with minor variations over the next two centuries. When Armenia became the first Christian kingdom – a few years before Constantine's conversion – it became more pro-Roman. It was finally divided between Persia and Rome in AD383, with Persia getting most of it.

Above: Arches of the aqueduct at Caesarea Maritima on the coast of Judaea (Israel) that were restored under Trajan.

Below: One of Herod the Great's proudest feats was the building of a Hellenized city at Caesarea Maritima with a huge Roman-style aqueduct.

AT THE EMPIRE'S EXTREMITIES
EGYPT

Above: The temple of Horus at Edfu is the only Egyptian temple to survive almost intact. The Romans continued to support the ancient priesthood to maintain the social status quo.

Below: The annual flooding of the Nile enriched its banks with silt brought down from central Africa, making it the chief granary of the ancient world. Egypt's grain went to feed the Roman populace after its conquest in 30BC.

When Octavian occupied Egypt after defeating Antony and Cleopatra in 30BC, he decided that this immensely rich, ancient and, to Roman eyes, strange land should become his personal property or private kingdom. This meant that the *princeps* became the heir of the Ptolemies, themselves heirs of nearly three millennia of pharaonic rule. Augustus was depicted and worshipped as a pharaoh. Later emperors at times restored or extended temples, as Trajan did at Philae, although the powers of priests were generally circumscribed. The Romans wanted Egypt as a granary for Rome.

Egypt, with a population of about eight million under the early Principate, was second only to Italy in size. A Praetorian prefect governed the province from Alexandria, and senators were forbidden to visit it without the emperor's express permission. The first prefect, Aelius Gallus, led a campaign deep into the Sudan, making grandiose claims for his conquests. This so angered Augustus that

Gallus was forced to commit suicide. Later prefects were more cautious, and the frontier remained fixed for centuries near Aswan. The bulk of the population, the *fellahin*, or peasants, were tied to their land and governed by a combination of priests and local bureaucrats, as they had been for millennia. Their forced labour continued to supply the wheat and other products – linen, cotton and papyrus, the precursor of paper found only along the Nile's banks – that now went to Rome rather than their own government; but for a long time they posed little problem. Most Egyptians paid the *laographia*, or special poll tax; only the three Greek cities – Alexandria, Ptolemais and Naucratis – were exempt. At first 27,000 troops – three legions plus auxiliaries – were kept to control the country, with a flotilla on the Nile, later reduced to just one legion (needed in turbulent Alexandria), for there was almost no external threat. The native Egyptians still spoke their ancient language, now known as Coptic, and were separate from the two newer populations, the Jews and the Greeks, whose disputes caused the Romans many problems.

Both Jews and Greeks had been in Egypt for some time. The first Jews had been settled by the Persians in the 6th century BC as military colonists around Old Babylon (Cairo), as the Persians were unpopular rulers in Egypt. When Alexander the Great founded Alexandria in 331BC, he invited Jews to settle there. Later, under the Ptolemies, whose empire stretched to the Lebanon, many Jews moved to the metropolis. By the 1st century BC, around 8–10 per cent of the population of Egypt was Jewish. Alexandria must have had a larger Jewish population than any city in Judaea itself. Many Jews prospered in Alexandria and, although they had their own quarters and kept their religion, some of them were influenced by Hellenism. Most famous of these was the philosopher Philo (*c*.25BC–AD45), whose attempts to reconcile the teachings of the Torah and Plato in works such as *The Contemplative Life* influenced later Christian thinking. Philo also took an active role in politics, leading the embassy of Jewish Alexandrians in AD40 to persuade Caligula not to enforce the worship of his own divinity on Jews. (Jews had been exempted from emperor-worship.) Caligula pronounced that those who could not see he was a god were more to be pitied than hated.

Philo's deputation to Rome was needed because of unceasing disputes and rivalries between Alexandria's Jews and its Greek-speakers, jealous of Jewish privileges. There were further riots between the two groups under Claudius. Under Nero, 50,000 people were killed when the Jews tried to burn down the amphitheatre and the governor had to send in two legions. In AD115 the whole Jewish population rose in revolt, causing immense destruction.

ALEXANDRIA: COSMOPOLIS AND CHRISTIAN CRADLE

With nearly one million inhabitants, Alexandria was almost as large as Rome under Augustus, and was still very much the centre of Greek scientific life. Heron invented the world's first steam engine there in the 1st century AD and Ptolemy drew up a map of the heavens a century later. Its famous library contained 500,000 papyrus rolls, the largest in the world, and its *pharos* (lighthouse), reputedly 400ft (120m) high, was the tallest structure in the world. Alexandria was the centre of trade routes stretching across the Mediterranean and east to India, its markets filled with exotic goods and peoples. Its grand boulevards, such as the Canopic Way lined with porticos, long eclipsed anything to be found in Rome. But it lacked what even the smallest *municipium* had: an elected council and magistrates.

This derived from the extremely autocratic government of the Ptolemies. Augustus continued without a council, which had to wait for Septimius Severus visiting Egypt in AD200–01. When the Alexandrians were not involved in commerce or sectarian strife, their thoughts turned to philosophy or religion. Plotinus, founder of antiquity's last great school of philosophy, was born there in AD204. But Egypt was also one of the most fertile grounds for early Christianity, which appealed both to native Egyptians and to erudite citizens of Alexandria.

The Greek theologian St Clement of Alexandria (*c*.AD150–214) was a bishop of Alexandria (later called Patriarchs). His pupil Origen (AD185–253), one of the first original Christian thinkers, castrated himself to avoid sexual temptation. Many early Christians went to the desert as a solution to this problem, with certain areas becoming almost crowded with hermits. Another Alexandrian bishop St Athanasius (AD295–373) attended the Council of Nicaea in AD325. Constantine accepted his views on the single nature of Christ, which became orthodox Christianity. Religious disputes continued to rack the city nearly as badly as the Greek–Jewish conflicts of earlier times.

Above: The Pharos of Alexandria was one of the Seven Wonders of the Ancient World. Reputedly 400ft (120m) high, it was the prototype of many such structures built by the Romans throughout their empire. This fanciful later picture understates its height.

Below: The bulk of the Egyptian population under the Romans remained fellahin, *or peasants, working the land and paying taxes mostly in kind. Only the advent of Christianity really affected them.*

AT THE EMPIRE'S EXTREMITIES
BRITAIN

Above: The ruins of Vindolanda, one of the many fine stone forts in Hadrian's wall country, built to mark the province's northern limits.

Below: Part of the Mildenhall Treasure, one of the most spectacular examples of Roman art in Britain, dating from the 4th century AD.

Although the English Channel formed one of the best natural frontiers the empire ever had, Britain had tantalized the Romans since Caesar's two brief expeditions of 55 and 54BC. The second, with five legions, had temporarily crushed some Britons, but did not lastingly affect its warring, if artistically gifted, Celtic tribes. Claudius, lacking a military background because of his disabilities, was eager to gain glory in this mysterious and reputedly rich island. Strabo had summed up Britain's exports as "hunting dogs, slaves, gold", but the Romans overestimated Britain's wealth. The cost of its large garrison – up to 30,000 troops – probably exceeded its revenues at first, but recent research suggests Britain contributed much more than was once thought to the empire.

The death in AD41 of Cunebolin (Shakespeare's Cymbeline), who had ruled much of south-east England from Camulodunum (Colchester), led to disputes between his sons, which helped the Romans. The invasion force of AD43 under Aulus Plautius, made up of four legions plus auxiliaries – about 40,000 men – landed at Richborough, moved north to the Thames, crushing all British resistance, then waited until Claudius hurriedly joined them before advancing. Claudius then established Camulodunum as the capital for his new province, and, hailed as *imperator* by his troops, proudly returned home.

Several client kingdoms acknowledged Roman suzerainty: the Iceni in Norfolk, the powerful Brigantes in northern England and the Regni in Sussex. The young general Vespasian led the Second Legion south-west, storming 20 *oppida* or hill forts. Meanwhile, the Ninth Legion moved north to Lincoln, which became a colony in the reign of Nerva (AD96–8). London, St Albans and other towns sprang up in the wake of the army in the AD70s, and the Fosse Way from Lincoln to Exeter marked in effect the first provisional boundary of Roman Britain.

This boundary proved temporary. Caratacus, one of Cunebolin's sons, escaped to rally opposition in Wales and drew the Romans west. Captured in AD51, he was taken in chains to Rome where he marvelled aloud that such a magnificent city should covet his poor land. Traditionally, Claudius, impressed by his courage, spared his life. A new governor, Suetonius Paulinus, decided to eliminate the Druid stronghold at Anglesey in AD58. The Romans rightly saw these priests, who practised human sacrifice, as inspiring British resistance. The revolt of the Iceni under Boudicca in AD60 made Suetonius Paulinus return in a hurry to crush them, but Roman policies were changed: the *publicani* were removed and a conciliatory attitude was adopted. Soon the burnt towns were rebuilt and British grandees began adopting Roman ways (as the near-palace at Fishbourne suggests), despite a total lack of imperial interest under Nero.

THE NORTHERN FRONTIER

The Brigantes, suddenly turning hostile under Venutius, their new king, were defeated at Stanwick in AD71, and Rome's northward advance resumed. Agricola, governor from AD77 to 83, encouraged the civilizing of lowland Britons, settling them in *civitates*, or towns, rather than hill forts, complete with theatres, forums and baths, and teaching them Latin. The Silures in Wales moved from their hill fortress to a new Roman town at Caerwent. Agricola then turned north to complete the conquest of the still mysterious island. He pushed deep into the Highlands, routing the assembled Caledonians at Mons Graupius (near Inverness), nearly completing the conquest of Britain. He then sent a fleet to circumnavigate the north and started to build a large legionary fortress at Inchtuthill, Tayside. It was never finished, for Agricola was soon recalled by Domitian and his northern forts were then abandoned.

When Hadrian visited Britain in AD122 he found the frontier in flux. True to his retractive instincts, he established a new 76-mile (122km) Tyne–Solway line. Intended to be permanent, it was built in stone in its eastern part, the western part being built initially in turf. In AD139, south Scotland was reoccupied and the turf Antonine Wall (named after emperor Antoninus) was built across the waist of Scotland along the Forth–Clyde line. It was abandoned by AD163, and Hadrian's Wall once again became the northern frontier. The emperor Septimius Severus marched north in AD209 and reached Aberdeen, but on his death in AD211 Scotland was again evacuated.

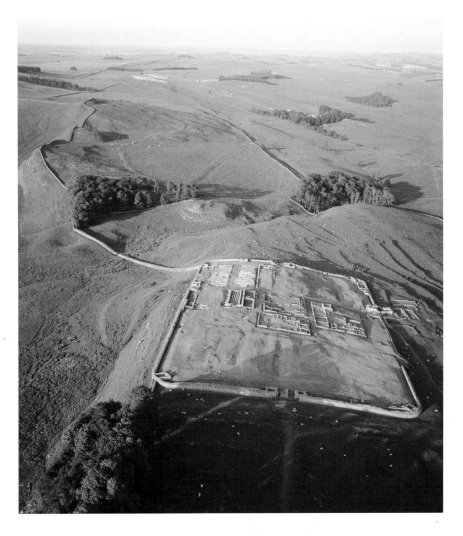

By AD130, a pattern of military garrisons had been established, with legionary forts at Chester, York and Caerleon and auxiliary troops along the walls and round Wales containing the still barbarous tribes. In lowland Britain urban life developed rapidly, if normally quite modestly. However, the great basilica and forum in London, built under Hadrian, were gigantic in size. The baths at Aquae Sulis (Bath) have an elegant opulence that suggests a sophisticated society, as does the large theatre at Verulamium (St Albans). Mining was developed – far more iron, lead and coal were produced than gold – along with farming and trade. Britain escaped the catastrophes of the 3rd century AD relatively lightly, although most towns now built themselves stone walls. But a new threat was emerging: Saxon raiders along the east coasts who would one day conquer the province.

Above: Housesteads was a typical fort on Hadrian's wall, with a garrison of one cohort of auxiliaries (c.500 men).

Below: A sea-god dominates the centre of a floor mosaic from a Romano–British villa. Such villas flourished up to the mid-4th century AD.

INDEX